Better Homes and Gardens®

Best of
Halloween
tricks & treats

WILEY

John Wiley & Sons, Inc.

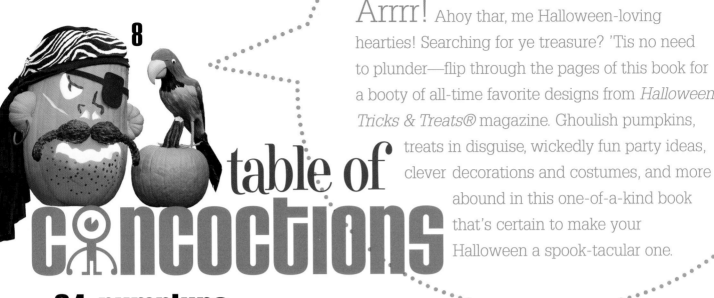

8

table of

CONCOCTIONS

Arrr! Ahoy thar, me Halloween-loving hearties! Searching for ye treasure? 'Tis no need to plunder—flip through the pages of this book for a booty of all-time favorite designs from *Halloween Tricks & Treats®* magazine. Ghoulish pumpkins, treats in disguise, wickedly fun party ideas, clever decorations and costumes, and more abound in this one-of-a-kind book that's certain to make your Halloween a spook-tacular one.

80

130

117

140

162

pumpkins

Halloween wouldn't be complete without good ol' Jack. Whether it's silly, ghoulish, jolly, or hauntingly unexpected, you'll find a pumpkin you'll want to carve and display in this collection.

DESIGNED BY WADE SCHERRER
WRITTEN BY LAURA HOLTORF COLLINS
PHOTOGRAPHED BY GREG SCHEIDEMANN

MAKING FACES

The spirit of creativity abounds in this jack-o'-lantern collection. Choose your favorite(s), and then check out the specific instructions and helpful carving tips that follow.

I'm Melting!

Looks like this wicked one has met her demise. Created from a warty pumpkin for the head and a gourd for the nose, this witch "collapses" into a large flowerpot draped with black fabric. Her hat, shoes, and broom can be found at theatrical shops.

Outdoor Apparitions
Here's an easy, inexpensive way to raise the spirit(s) of the season. These ethereal shapes are done with minimal carving, tall dowel rods, and sheets of breezy cheesecloth.

Dynamic Duo
Forget bad luck—this painted black cat with glowing carved eyes and lit-up moon will be a welcome sight along anyone's path tonight. Pair the feline with a jolly pumpkin pal to greet your trick-or-treaters.

Avast, Mateys!
What gives this swashbuckler such character? Is it his eye patch or the scar on his cheek? Maybe it's his mustache and ears crafted from mini gourds. All of these details—and many more—will delight anyone who rings your doorbell tonight.

Skull-fully Carved

Heads served on a silver platter—how fiendishly fun! Cut from white pumpkins about the size of human heads, this trio, *above,* "floats" in midair when you rest each carved head atop a clear shallow bowl. Crafts-foam bow ties, pinned at the necks, make it a formal affair.

Drats! Rats!

Painted rodents gather 'round the big CHEESE for this glow-in-the-dark assemblage, *below*. Cutouts carved into the tall pumpkin let out plenty of candlelight, but outlines gouged around each rat silhouette emit only an eerie flicker.

Bats in the Belfry

Take a fresh bite into your pumpkin carving this Halloween, *right*. Instead of cutting off the top for a lid, remove the bottom from the pumpkin and clean it out. Then use the two bat patterns on *page 16* to create a fanged grin and a hair-raising hairline.

Tombstone Territory

Turn a corner of your patio or your front yard into a haunted graveyard, *below*. This one is filled with lighted headstones and body parts that rise from the ground.

Halloween Dudes

This pair goes dapper when you add top hats and a fringed ascot to the picture, *opposite*. To give the fellow on the right a piercing look, insert metal bottle caps into carved eye circles.

Pumpkin-Carving Basics

MATERIALS

- Fresh or carvable artificial pumpkin
- Tracing paper
- Tape or straight pins
- Tools: apple corer, paring knife, grapefruit spoon, mixing spoon, crafts knife; pumpkin carving tools (including assorted saws, drills, poker, and scoop); clay tools (for engraving and cutting grooves); wood-carving set (including gouges)
- For fresh pumpkin only: petroleum jelly, flat-edge ice cream scoop or large serving spoon

PREPARE FRESH PUMPKIN

Allow your pumpkin to come to room temperature. Draw the outline of a round lid on top of the pumpkin. Then draw a notch at the back to use as a guide for replacing the lid. Make the lid large enough to let you easily clean out the pumpkin. Instead of cutting a lid, you may wish to draw a round opening on the bottom of the pumpkin. With the bottom removed, the pumpkin can sit over a candle or a light.

Cut out the lid or bottom opening with a saw or a knife. To cut out a lid, carve at an angle toward the pumpkin center. This creates a ledge to support the lid. To cut out a bottom opening, cut straight into the base (*photo 1, below*).

Clean out the seeds and pulp with a spoon (*photo 2, below*). Scrape the pulp from the area you plan to carve until the pumpkin wall is about 1 inch thick (*photo 3, below*).

GENERAL INSTRUCTIONS

Enlarge or decrease your pattern to fit your pumpkin. Attach the pattern to your pumpkin using tape or straight pins. If you use pins, place them on the design lines to avoid unwanted holes in the pumpkin.

For a fresh pumpkin, use a poker tool to make holes along the design lines about $\frac{1}{8}$ inch apart (*photo 4, below*).

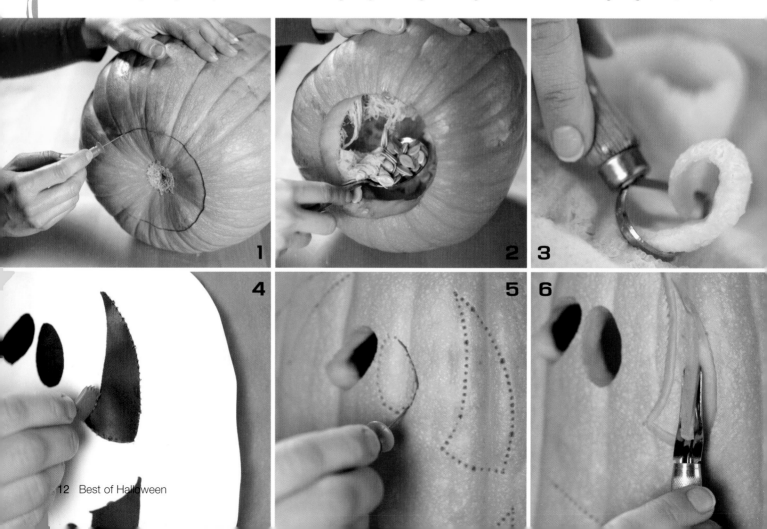

Don't push the poker through the wall of the pumpkin. Remove the pattern when finished. For an artificial pumpkin, use a pencil to draw firmly over the pattern and engrave the design lines on the pumpkin skin.

Cradle the pumpkin in your lap, and use a crafts knife or a saw to begin cutting out the design *(photo 5, opposite)*. For smaller, more intricate openings, be sure to use a fine-tooth saw. Grasp the saw as you would hold a pencil and cut with a continuous up-and-down motion, keeping the saw perpendicular to the pumpkin. Apply only gentle pressure to avoid breaking the knife or saw blade and to guard against stressing or breaking the pumpkin. To avoid putting pressure on areas already carved, work from the center of the design outward. Remove and reinsert the knife to make corners; don't twist the blade. Use your finger to carefully push the pieces out of the pumpkin.

To create an interesting design with color and light, you can remove the skin of the pumpkin after cutting out all openings. Use a rounded gouge, assorted clay tools, grapefruit spoon, or crafts knife to remove the skin and pulp to the thickness desired *(photo 6, opposite)*.

Use an electric or battery-powered light in an artificial pumpkin; do not use a candle. To use a candle inside a fresh pumpkin, place the candle inside and carefully light it after all carving is completed. After the candle smoke has blackened a spot on the lid or the top, use a saw to cut a 1-inch-diameter hole at that spot for a chimney.

To reduce shriveling, coat the cut edges of your carving with petroleum jelly. You can revive a shriveled pumpkin by soaking it in water for 1-8 hours. After removing it from the water, let it drain and air-dry.

I'm Melting! Witch Cutout

Note: See Pumpkin-Carving Basics, including a list of tools, tips, and techniques such as transferring your pattern, opposite.

Select a round pumpkin with plenty of warts. Transfer the eye and mouth patterns onto the pumpkin. Using a knife or carving tools, cut out the openings.

Cut the end off a gourd to be used as a nose. Insert a wood skewer into the nose and then push it into the pumpkin to hold the nose in place.

Drape a piece of black fabric over a large upright flowerpot. (The flowerpot should be large enough to support the pumpkin.) Set the pumpkin on the fabric-covered flowerpot. Place a black witch's hat on the pumpkin. Pin the hat to the pumpkin if necessary. Tuck an old broom and witch's shoes so they're poking out from under the fabric.

Halloween-Dudes Cutouts

Note: For Pumpkin-Carving Basics, including a list of tools, tips, and techniques such as transferring your pattern, turn to page 12.

Transfer the patterns onto the pumpkins. Using a knife or carving tools, cut out the openings. Add top hats. (Ours came from a theatrical shop.) Tie a fringed scarf around the base of one pumpkin for a cravat. Insert two metal bottle caps into the circle eyes for the other pumpkin.

Drats! Rats! Cutouts

Note: For Pumpkin-Carving Basics, including a list of tools, tips, and techniques such as transferring your pattern, turn to page 12.

Transfer the letters and Swiss–cheese holes onto one large pumpkin. Using a knife or carving tools, cut out the openings.

Spray the pumpkin with varnish so paint will adhere to the pumpkin. Transfer the rat patterns onto smaller pumpkins. Use a gouge to cut a thin outline around the rats, cutting just deep enough to let the glow of a candle escape through the pumpkin's walls. Paint the rat silhouettes with black acrylic paint. Spray with varnish to seal the paint.

Bats-in-the-Belfry Vampire Cutout

Note: For Pumpkin-Carving Basics, including a list of tools, tips, and techniques such as transferring your pattern, turn to page 12.

Transfer the eyes and bat patterns onto the pumpkin, referring to the photo, *page 10*, for placement. Using a knife or carving tools, cut out the openings.

Avast, Mateys! Pirate Cutout

Note: For Pumpkin-Carving Basics, including a list of tools, tips, and techniques such as transferring your pattern, turn to page 12.

Cut a longneck gourd (for the mustache) and a mini pumpkin (for the ears) in half lengthwise with a hacksaw. Drill a hole into one ear to hold a curtain-rod ring for the earring.

Referring to the photo, *page 8*, decide on the placement for the mustache and temporarily mark its position. Transfer the eye, nostrils, scar, and scowl patterns onto the pumpkin. Using a knife or carving tools, cut out the openings.

Attach the mustache and ears to the pumpkin with toothpicks. *(Note: Color any toothpick ends that show with marking pens.)*

Freehand-draw the eye, nose, and whisker details using a black permanent marking pen.

Transfer the eye-patch pattern onto tracing paper and use it to cut the shape from black crafts foam. Use toothpicks to secure the ends of the eye patch to the pumpkin.

Create a bandanna with scraps of fabric, and add the earring.

Tombstone Territory Cutouts

Note: For Pumpkin-Carving Basics, including a list of tools, tips, and techniques such as transferring your pattern, turn to page 12.

Transfer the patterns onto the pumpkins. Using a knife or carving tools, cut out the openings.

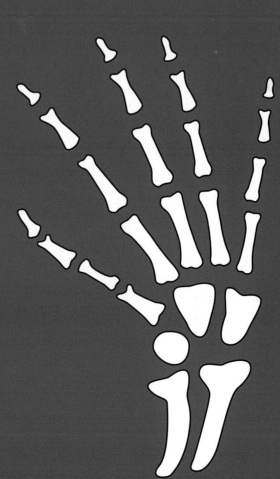

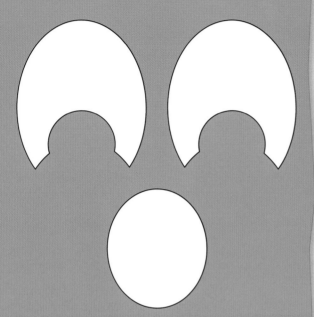

Outdoor Apparitions Cutout

Note: For Pumpkin-Carving Basics, including a list of tools, tips, and techniques such as transferring your pattern, turn to page 12.

Transfer the mouth and eye patterns onto the pumpkin, referring to the photo, *page 7*, for placement. Using a knife or carving tools, cut out the mouth opening and then clean out the pumpkin through the mouth. Cut out the eyes.

Hammer a 1-inch-diameter, 4-foot length of dowel rod into the ground until it is deep enough to securely hold a pumpkin. Using a 7/8-inch drill bit, drill a hole in the bottom of the pumpkin. Push the pumpkin onto the top of the rod. Mark the rod 1 inch below the head. Remove the pumpkin.

For arms, remove and discard the hook from a clothes hanger. Straighten the remaining hanger wire. On your mark, drill a small hole (to accommodate the wire) crosswise through the dowel rod. Thread the wire through the hole and wrap it around once for stability. Bend the ends into circles so they won't snag the cheesecloth. Drape a length of cheesecloth from the front to the back and another (shorter) length from side to side.

Skull-fully Carved Pumpkin Cutout

Note: For Pumpkin-Carving Basics, including a list of tools, tips, and techniques such as transferring your pattern, turn to page 12.

Transfer the skull pattern onto the pumpkin. Using a knife or carving tools, cut out the openings.

Trace a bow-tie shape onto tracing paper, and use it to cut out a shape from black crafts foam (available at crafts stores). Cut a short, narrow strip of black crafts foam for the bow-tie center. Wrap and glue the band around the center of the bow tie. Push one or two toothpicks through the center of the bow tie to attach it to the pumpkin.

Bonus

Jolly Pumpkin

Note: For Pumpkin-Carving Basics, including a list of tools, tips, and techniques such as transferring your pattern, turn to page 12.

Transfer patterns onto pumpkins and cut out the openings with a knife or carving tools. *Tip: Download pumpkin features from bhg.com/pumpkinstencil. Visit the site to design your own creations!*

Black Cat Pumpkin

Note: For Pumpkin-Carving Basics, including a list of tools, tips, and techniques such as transferring your pattern, turn to page 12.

Spray the pumpkin with spray varnish so paint will adhere to the pumpkin. Transfer the pattern onto the pumpkin and cut out the eyes and the moon with a knife or carving tools. Paint the cat with black acrylic paint and an artist's brush that best fits the area. Dip the handle end of the brush into white acrylic paint and apply dip-dots to the pumpkin for the necklace. Let the paint dry thoroughly. Spray with varnish to seal the paint.

Carved, painted, or adorned with embellishments, our parade of pumpkins

PUMPKIN GALLERY

DESIGNED BY ROBERTA ROYCE   PHOTOGRAPHED BY ANDY LYONS   WRITTEN BY PATRICIA GARRINGTON

will inspire you to create your own haunting Halloween display.

Create a collection of carved and decorated pumpkins that spell out a word or phrase. For more fun, also include both scary and silly silhouettes.

Haunted Mansion

Chisel windows in a painted mansion and add a carved moon behind, *opposite.* Candlelight from inside the pumpkin will bring the night to life.

Frightfully-Fun Feline

Fashion a wide-eyed cat, *top right,* to lurk on a porch or in a garden to greet those who dare to trespass. Carve the face, attach chenille stems for whiskers and crafts-foam cutouts for ears, and watch a friendly feline appear as if by magic.

Spine-Chilling Spider

The painted sinister spider dangling on a luminous web warns visitors to beware, *bottom right.* The lines of the web are carved just deep enough to let the glow of the candle shine through the pumpkin walls.

Light Up the Sky
Paint several bats in flight and then carve silhouettes of a moon and stars for illumination, *top left.*

Grinning Ghouls
A row of shepherd's hooks set along the sidewalk is a perfect way to display tiny jack-o'-lantern luminaries and to light the way to your house, *bottom left.* Use heavy-gauge wire to create sturdy hangers; then insert a hanger into the top of each pumpkin.

Creepy Crow
When summer fades to autumn and songbirds start to fly south, a birdbath becomes a perfect perch for a pumpkin painted with a macabre crow, *opposite.* A coat of varnish protects the pumpkin from the elements.

Pumpkin Face Cutouts

Note: For Pumpkin Carving Basics, including a list of tools, tips, and techniques such as transferring your pattern, turn to page 12.

Transfer the face patterns onto the pumpkins and cut out the openings with a knife or carving tools.

Spooky Spider Cutout

Note: For Pumpkin-Carving Basics, including a list of tools, tips, and techniques such as transferring your pattern, turn to page 12.

Spray the pumpkin with spray varnish so paint will adhere to the pumpkin. Transfer the patterns onto the pumpkin. Use a gouge to carve ¼ inch into the skin for the web. Paint the spider with black acrylic paint and an artist's brush. Let the paint dry. Spray with varnish to seal the paint.

Boo Cutouts

Note: For Pumpkin-Carving Basics, including a list of tools, tips, and techniques such as transferring your pattern, turn to page 12.

Transfer the patterns onto the pumpkins. Use a gouge to carve ¼ inch into the skin on the pattern lines for each letter.

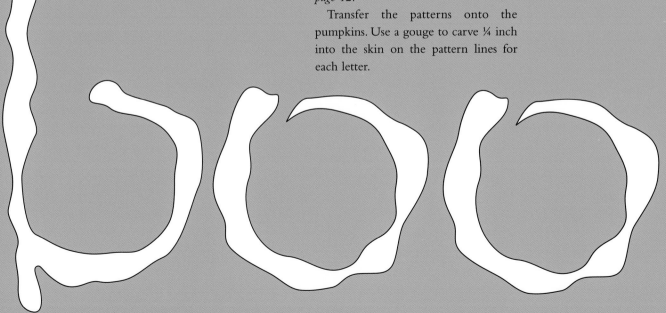

Bonus

Smiley Face
Cutout

*Note: For Pumpkin-Carving
Basics, including a list of tools,
tips, and techniques such as
transferring your pattern, turn
to page 12.*

Transfer the face pattern
onto the pumpkins and cut
out the openings with a
knife or carving tools.

Haunted Mansion and
Light Up the Sky Cutouts

Note: For Pumpkin-Carving Basics, including a list of tools, tips, and techniques such as transferring your pattern, turn to page 12.

Spray the pumpkin with spray varnish so paint will adhere to the pumpkin. Transfer the patterns onto the pumpkins and cut out the openings with a knife. Paint the bats, *opposite,* or house with black acrylic paint and an artist's brush that best fits the area. Let the paint dry thoroughly. Spray with varnish to seal the paint.

Creepy Crow

Note: For Pumpkin-Carving Basics, including a list of tools, tips, and techniques such as transferring your pattern, turn to page 12.

Spray the pumpkin with spray varnish so paint will adhere to the pumpkin. Transfer the pattern onto the pumpkin. Paint the design with black acrylic paint and an artist's brush that best fits the area. Let the paint dry. Spray with varnish to seal the paint. Insert a pearl-head pin into the pumpkin for the crow's eye.

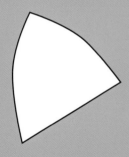

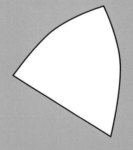

Frightfully-Fun Feline Cutout

Note: For Pumpkin-Carving Basics, including a list of tools, tips, and techniques, such as transferring your pattern, turn to page 12.

Transfer the patterns onto the pumpkin and cut out the openings with a knife. Cut three black chenille stems in half. Poke two small holes under the cat's nose and insert the chenille stems. Cut ear shapes from black crafts foam and secure in place with hotmelt adhesive.

Grinning Ghouls Cutouts

(small hanging luminaries)

Note: For Pumpkin-Carving Basics, including a list of tools, tips, and techniques such as transferring your pattern, turn to page 12.

Choose small pumpkins of similar size that are large enough to accommodate a small candle. Transfer the face patterns onto the pumpkins and cut out the openings with a knife or carving tools. Cut lengths of heavy gauge black crafts wire and bend; poke the ends inside each pumpkin on either side to form a handle. Twist the ends inside the pumpkin to keep the handle secure.

out of your gourd!

DESIGNS: STAFF PHOTOGRAPHER: SCOTT LITTLE

Whether the atmosphere you aim for is goofy or ghostly, silly or scary, a trip to the farmer's market or produce aisle in your local market will yield all the ingredients to create these organic designs.

curly locks

The simply carved features on this pumpkin are perfect for an amateur carver. A quarter-moon mouth is studded with garlic-clove teeth and each arched eye is filled with a radish; all are attached with florist's pins. Use an apple corer to drill holes for hair and ear placement; fill in with broccoli-stalk hair and artichoke ears. The gargantuan gourd nose is held in place with toothpicks.

crack 'em up

After a few simple facial features are cut out, this wrinkly dude's face is gouged with jagged cracks. The connected cuts give the face a river of wrinkles. His bad-hair-day look comes from a shock of willow branches (choose dried ones from a crafts store or fresh ones from the garden). Small holes drilled into the head allow for easy insertion of the branches.

bird haven

This funny fellow is all ears! To make these elephant-size examples, saw a large gourd in half from stem to stern; securely attach each ear to the head with two florist's pins. A dab of red glass paint on the front of a glass landscape bubble forms the beacon nose. Insert the bubble nose into a hole cut just the right size; when the pumpkin is lit, the nose will glow red. For the eyes, pin a radish into the top of each egg-shape eye. A coiled-moss-nest hat positioned at a rakish angle makes a soft spot for a bird to nest on jumbo garlic-clove eggs. The bird is cleverly constructed from a gourd with clove-studded eyes and a green onion tail (drill a small hole in the back end of the gourd and insert the head of the onion).

are you my mummy?

To make a pumpkin "mummy," locate two areas, one for an eye and one for a mouth; then work the "wrappings" around these two places. To begin the pattern, cut and place sections of masking tape on the pumpkin, leaving a narrow uncovered strip between the tape sections, until you've covered the pumpkin. Leave pumpkin skin visible at all crossings of the wrapped sections. Use a pencil to mark along the edges of the tape; then, one section at a time, remove the tape and use a V-shape gouge to remove the skin. Use assorted gouges to remove all skin where the tape was. Work one section at a time. When all the wraps are carved, cut out the mouth and the eye openings. Use paint pens to turn a glass landscape bubble into an eye. Insert the eye into the opening. Pin several garlic cloves inside the mouth opening.

stand-up comedian

This upstanding character will greet passersby with a huge grin and a hat to match. Cut out the facial features; then add radishes to star-shape eyes. Drill holes in the head to hold cauliflower hair. For the nose, drill a hole to fit the narrow end of a gourd. For the gourd hat, cut an opening in the pumpkin top. Lay pieces of kale on top of the opening, and place the gourd on the hole, securing the kale in place. Tie a ribbon around the "hat." Place the finished pumpkin in an iron sculpture that gives the clown "body" (see Sources, page 191).

curly locks

crack 'em up

bird haven

stand-up comedian

GRINNING GOURDS

Once a year, accomplished potter Steve Steininger turns into a passionate pumpkin carver. From grinning politicians to toothy-faced creatures with devilish smiles, his pumpkin art takes jack-o'-lanterns one step above the rest. As he waits each fall for gourds, Steininger takes inspiration for his pumpkin creations from faces, pottery, and sculpture. Although his carvings look intricate, his technique for creating fiendish faces is easy enough for almost anyone to tackle.

WRITER: JUDITH STERN FRIEDMAN PHOTOGRAPHER: ANDY LYONS

Steve Steininger is a magician of sorts, creating a spirited show of pumpkins that appears one day and vanishes at season's end—which is probably why most of his pumpkins cry. With his first cut into the cool orange rind, a drop of liquid trickles down the fruit's cheek. "This is going to hurt a little bit," Steve warns as a crowd of people gathers to watch him carve.

Today, he's working at ArtFest Midwest, a local art fair in Des Moines, Iowa, churning out little jack-o'-lanterns to give away to the kids. Guided by faces the children themselves have drawn, Steve quickly carves the gourds and gives them to the kids to decorate with paints or markers.

Until now, he's been waiting eagerly for the first pumpkins of the harvest. "As soon as I can find a pumpkin in the store, I start carving," he says, usually taking from 15 minutes to an hour for each, although some designs can take all day. Steve's artistry revolves around his special carving technique that penetrates only the surface of the pumpkin's skin. Small beveled cuts form intricate lines that allow him to fashion elaborate face details.

A SIGHT TO SEE

"The eyes are the soul of the pumpkin," Steve says. "They're the most important feature for creating scariness."

Squinting, sneering, sneaky, or surprised, each pair of peepers is a visual spectacle. Then the rest of the face falls into place, he says. He chisels in wrinkles, a billowy nose, and a big mean mouth that screams with delight. Occasionally, a mustache, a goatee, or a pair of wicked brows intensifies the sinister expression. "I keep finding more details to add," Steve says. "It's so much fun to do—I don't want it to end."

Though Steve just lets his carving take its course (he typically doesn't sketch before he cuts), he's always studying faces for inspiration. A full-time artist and potter by trade, he collects pottery, which includes pre-Columbian motifs, and he visits museums to examine primitive sculptures. He seeks out African carvings, Japanese masks, and Polynesian and New Zealand art that often bear grimaces he can transfer to his ghouls.

Specific faces with distinct features lend themselves

"They're HERE and then they're GONE," Steve says of his short-lived works of ART.

His impressive, attention-getting gourds laugh typical carved designs straight out of the pumpkin patch. Because his globes are hollowed out from the bottom, the curly stems remain intact, adding to the pumpkins' uniqueness. And since only the surface is scraped, the thin rind casts a soft, almost eerie glow when light shines through from behind it. Steve's pumpkins cackle, connive, and brew up a stir that he is happy to share with the crowd.

to caricatures. And sometimes real life offers models: For example, one Halloween he carved several pumpkin pairs of 2004 presidential candidates George Bush and John Kerry. One set went to a downtown Des Moines steak house, which then held a "straw poll" using cocktail straws.

TAKING A STAB

Steve insists that as hard as it looks, the carving method is easy. "Pumpkin is easy to carve," says Steve. "There's no grain to grab your knife and direct it away. It's a lot like carving in cold butter."

ABOVE LEFT: As he creates his intricate faces, Steve likes to hold the pumpkin on his lap so he can roll it around as he carves the expression, which usually extends around half of the pumpkin. **ABOVE RIGHT:** Sneaky eyes and a curly goatee suggest this pumpkin's up to something. **RIGHT:** Prop your pumpkins outside to catch the autumn chill. The cooler you keep them, the longer they last. (Be careful to avoid freezing, though, or they'll lose their shape upon thawing.) **BELOW:** Instead of cutting entirely through the rind, use a crafts knife to gouge V-shape beveled pieces from the pumpkin's surface.

Ten-pound pumpkins are best, Steve says, because they're easy to grip between the knees and roll around in the lap. He also looks for twisted, curvy stems for added interest. First, using a kitchen butcher knife, he slices off the bottom so the pumpkin sits level. Because of the way he carves, Steve could leave the insides of the pumpkin intact. Instead, he uses a large metal spoon or ice cream scoop as his tool of choice for scraping out the guts. Not only is the light quality better with the insides clean, Steve says, but pumpkins last longer with the moisture removed. To extend the lives of his pumpkins, Steve has begun to explore preservation techniques, including (appropriately!) mummification.

To create a pumpkin using Steve's technique, he advises carvers to first decide which area of the pumpkin to cut, based on the best angle for viewing the stem. A crafts knife is all he uses to define the expressive facial features. "Most of the time, you're cutting through the surface just a little bit," Steve

CARVING A NICHE

Steve has carved pumpkins for about 10 years. When he was young, he didn't carve anything other than standard triangle eyes and noses on his pumpkins. He credits his talent to his art-teacher mother; Steve also taught art for three years before realizing he needed to create on his own. So he went to work for a potter, a woman named Karen, whom he married a few years later. Now Steve and Karen throw and fire their own functional stoneware, including clay pumpkins that they sell nationwide.

While carving real pumpkins is mostly for pleasure (he carves some pumpkins on commission), Steve loves the diversion during these few weeks of the year. He sends spirited carved samples to his children's teachers and delivers fiendish faces to local establishments. He has also started his own pumpkin patch to experiment with growing unusual gourd shapes while also seeking new ways to make his monsters last.

Still, Steve isn't saddened by his pumpkins' short lives.

"The EYES are the SOUL of the pumpkin. They're the most important FEATURE for creating SCARINESS."

explains. Rather than gouging out chunks of rind, he cuts small beveled V-shapes and pops out the pieces, exposing the light yellow meat underneath, rolling and turning the pumpkin as he works.

Finishing requires a quick wet "wipe down." Then Steve inserts Christmas lights or a lightbulb socket, as these are safer and cast a cooler glow than traditional votives or candles.

He's already conjuring up ideas for next Halloween's crop. And as he wipes the tear from his first incision on this day, he knows the fine figure will bring joy to fellow lovers of jack-o'-lanterns.

ABOVE LEFT: Tools of the potter's trade include scrapers and knives of various sorts, but all Steve uses for his pumpkin designs is a crafts knife. **ABOVE RIGHT:** Steve also transfers autumn-inspired designs onto "pumpkins" of clay. **RIGHT:** Steve carves pumpkins mostly for fun; it's a fall activity that lends itself well to his trade as a potter. Notice the intact top on this grinning gourd; Steve cuts a slice off the bottom of the pumpkin to scrape the inside clean.

parties

The secret to a great Halloween party? Plenty of tricks and treats! Conjure up your own successful soirée with these fun-loving ideas for kids, families, and adults alike.

SOMETHING OLD
SOMETHING NEW
A Halloween Party
WITH A WEDDING SKEW!

HALLO WEDDING

Scare up some fun this Halloween with a party that's like a wickedly haunted wedding reception. You'll say 'I do' to our cheeky ideas.

PRODUCTION ASSISTANT HOLLY RAIBIKIS   PAPER PROJECTS DESIGNED BY ONE HEART... ONE MIND   FOOD STYLED BY JILL LUST
WRITTEN BY BECKY MOLLENKAMP   PHOTOGRAPHED BY GREG SCHEIDEMANN

Invitation to Disaster

Cast a spell on your guests with a torn and tattered invitation, *opposite right*. Printed on a vellum overlay with a ripped edge, the invitation is aged with black ink and accented with a blood-red tassel.

Fa-boo-lous Feast

Send the signal that this is no ordinary buffet with an eerie table covering conjured from yards of gauzy cheesecloth. Frosting is your adhesive when you cover a witch-shaped hat with cookies of your choice. Add more goth to your background by burning purchased candles that drip "blood" and a grouping of frames aged with black paint.

Take the Cake

Typically the center of attention at a wedding, the cake table, *above,* puts a spooky spin on tradition. A card table is covered in muslin and edged with black tulle gathered into swags held by ribbon loops. The "cake" is a trio of paper-covered hatboxes aged with paint. Black-painted mums, doily napkins, and nut-filled espresso cups finish off the display.

Nail in the Coffin

For an appropriately creepy take-home treat, fill favor boxes with candy bones, *top left.* Give the boxes a casket look by weathering the edges with chalk, adding press-on letters and stick-on gems, and then tying them with ribbon.

Parting Shot

Send guests home with another grim reminder of your party, *middle left.* Take their photos with the Grim Reaper behind an oversize frame. Give the pics as unique favors.

The Happy Couple

Top the "cake" with a pair of plastic skeletons, *bottom left,* embellished with felt and tulle wedding-attire accents and a ring of blood-red roses with black-painted leaves.

MAKE A SOLEMN VOW TO FRIGHTEN YOUR friends with a haunted party that's a wedding reception. This creepy-crawly get-together gently pokes fun at tradition by putting an ominous spin on wedding customs.

The party's black, white, and blood-red color scheme starts with an invitation that asks guests to come to the event in their scariest wedding attire. (Who says you can never wear that hideous bridesmaid's gown again?) Host and hostess play the roles of corpse bride and groom, while a friend comes as the Grim Reaper, who will serve as master of ceremonies for the night.

Give the party room the look of an abandoned haunted house by clearing out the space and then dressing it in layers of aged, cobwebbed decor. We used a spirited mix of paper and fabric projects, aged accents, and painted flowers to set our scene.

Add to the fear factor with a silly menu of Halloween-theme foods. Our hair-raising buffet includes tombstone chicken-salad sandwiches, skeleton-bone pretzel sticks, fudgy graveyard gravel, a witch's hat made of cookies, and eyeball punch.

From start to finish, this clever event is (wedded) bliss that comes sealed with a kiss—of doom!

Ghoulish Gifts
Every wedding reception has a gift table. For the macabre display *above,* paper-covered boxes are filled with the usual trappings (a toaster and blender) as well as an unexpected surprise (a skull).

Book of Love
Keep up tradition with a guest book, *right.* Burn the edges of paper and age the pages with splatters of ink. Place a feather into the top of a pen and place it into a vintage-look stand made with paper-covered wood findings. Preprinted acetate with a spiderweb design trims a lampshade. Then finish with a welcome message on a framed piece of plywood painted with chalkboard paint.

Give baked brie the sinister treatment by topping it with "guts" made of sun-dried tomatoes, basil, and onions, *top right*. Served with French bread, the soft cheese is a sophisticated treat.

Gruesome Gourds

Serve up a variety of delicious dips, including Walnut-Feta Yogurt and Red Pepper, in glass dishes inserted into hollowed-out latex pumpkins, *middle right*. For extra fright, place plastic spiders among the dips, chips, crackers, and vegetables.

Demon Drink

Toast the happy couple with a wicked brew, *below*. The special Coconut Snowball Martini—concocted of white chocolate, coconut, cream, rum, and vodka—is served with red cake gel around the rim. The cocktail table also includes chilled champagne and oysters on the half shell.

SEND SHUDDERS DOWN GUESTS' SPINES WITH A MENACING MENU OF DELICIOUSLY DREADFUL TRICKS AND TREATS.

Hands Down
Guests will do a double take with this creepy-crawly finger food, *above.* Dip large pretzel sticks into white candy coating and add "nails" with slivered almonds. Display the fingers in a cuff-covered jar.

Buried Alive
The chicken-and-pecan salad sandwiches, *left,* are cut into tombstone shapes, rolled in chopped pecans for the look of stone, and displayed in a graveyard with creepy cabbage groundcover.

For instructions and recipes, see page 56.

Party Invitation to Disaster

THE PLEASURE OF YOUR COMPANY IS REQUESTED
SATURDAY, THE TWENTY~SEVENTH OF OCTOBER,
TWO THOUSAND AND SEVEN,
AT EIGHT O'CLOCK IN THE EVENING

At the Smith Manse
❦ 123 HICKORY LANE ❧

JOIN US FOR THE UNION OF TWO CLASSIC PARTY THEMES:
A HALLOWEEN BASH AND A WEDDING RECEPTION
(WE'LL HAVE WICKEDLY TASTY POTIONS, CONCOCTIONS & ELIXIRS)

Costume theme
FORMAL WEAR FORMERLY WORN

page 50

MATERIALS

  8½×11-inch sheet of white card stock

  Black-and-white patterned papers (We used two chandelier patterns in the Formality Collection from One Heart … One Mind.)

  Clear vellum

  Double-sided tape

  Glue dots

  Red tasseled cording

INSTRUCTIONS

Fold card stock in half to measure 5½×8½ inches.

Cut two 5¼×8¼-inch rectangles from the patterned papers. Adhere one to the front of the card and the other to the inside.

Using assorted fonts, plan the lettering to fit the front of the invitation (see page 50). Print the words on a piece of vellum. Cut out the vellum, tearing it along one edge. Adhere it to the front of the invitation with tiny glue dots.

For the inside, shown at *left,* use assorted fonts and plan the lettering for the party details to fit the same space used for the front of the invitation. Print the words on vellum. Cut out and adhere it to the inside of the invitation. Wrap and knot the cording around the fold.

Faux Candelabra *page 51*

MATERIALS

  Plastic foam (We used Floral Styrofoam.)

  Plastic-foam cutter (We used FloraCraft Styro Wonder Cutter Plus.)

  Straight pins

  Crafts knife

  Metal ruler

  Crafts glue

  Masking tape

  Black spray paint (We used Krylon flat black.)

  Wooden toothpicks

  3-inch wooden craft picks

  Heat gun

INSTRUCTIONS

Enlarge the patterns to your desired size. Cut out the patterns and pin them to the foam. With black paint, spray the patterns to create pattern silhouettes. Remove the patterns to reveal the candelabra shapes.

With a crafts knife, cut away the excess foam in the larger sections. *Note*: If a piece of foam breaks, add a generous amount of glue, place toothpicks or craft picks into one side of the break, and then press the other section back into place. Hold the pieces together with masking tape until the glue dries.

With the heated foam cutter, cut the curved shapes on each foam piece. Use a metal ruler and crafts knife to cut the straight lines, such as the taper shapes. A piece of scrap foam will serve as sandpaper to sand areas smooth if needed. For added strength, insert craft picks into curved areas, pushing the picks below the foam surface.

With the heat gun, heat all foam surfaces until you hear a sizzle, indicating that the foam has shrunk slightly and become stiffer.

Apply a generous amount of glue to the center cutout areas and gently slide the two foam pieces together to form the candelabra. Apply tape until the glue dries.

In a well-ventilated area, apply several light coats of paint, allowing drying time between coats.

Wedding Ghosts (Guests) Book *page 53*

MATERIALS

Corrugated cardboard: 7½×12-inch
piece (front); 9×12-inch piece (back);
and 1½×12-inch strip (binding)

Black-and-white patterned papers (We
used items in the Formality
Collection from One Heart … One
Mind.)

Card stock: black and light gray

Kraft paper (for pages)

Walnut ink and paintbrush

"GUESTS" title label (We used Bits-n-
Pieces from One Heart … One Mind.)

Double-sided tape

Red tasseled cord

INSTRUCTIONS

For the book front, cover one side of
the 7½×12-inch cardboard piece with
patterned paper; add a 1½×12-inch strip
of contrasting patterned paper along the
left edge. Adhere the piece to a 12×12-
inch piece of gray card stock with the
right edges aligned. A 1½-inch margin
of gray card stock should extend from
the left edge. Wrap a 4×12-inch piece
of black card stock around the binding
strip, overlapping the long edges on the
wrong side. Tape this covered strip to the
gray margin.

For the book back, cover one side
of 9×12-inch cardboard piece with
patterned paper and the other side with
light gray card stock.

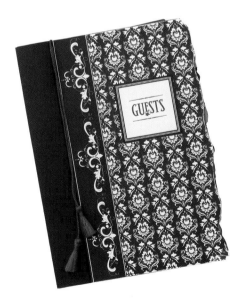

Spiderweb Lampshade

page 53

MATERIALS

Lampshade

Spiderweb printed acetate (Ours is
from Hambly.)

Spray adhesive

INSTRUCTIONS

Make a tracing paper pattern for one
side of the lampshade. Lay the pattern
atop the acetate, and cut out the shape
with scissors or a crafts knife.

Spray the acetate with the adhesive
and press onto the shade.

Groom's Corsage

page 54

MATERIALS

Chipboard flowers: 1¾- and 3-inch-
diameter

Two black-and-white patterned papers

Black acrylic paint and paintbrush

Spray adhesive

Glue gun and hotmelt adhesive

¾-inch-diameter black-and-white
button

Pinback

6-inch square of black netting

INSTRUCTIONS

Trace each chipboard flower onto a
patterned paper. Cut out the shapes.

Paint the edges of the chipboard
flowers black; let dry.

Adhere the paper flowers to the
chipboard flowers using spray adhesive.

Use hot glue to assemble the rest of
the corsage as follows: adhere the small
flower to the large flower and a button
for the flower center. Attach a pinback
to the back. Fold the netting in quarters;
gather one edge of the folded netting,
securing the gathers with a needle and
thread. Glue the gathered edge below
the pinback.

Using a crafts knife, make an irregular cut along the right long edges of the book front and the book back.

Using a computer or an adhesive alphabet, add "GUESTS" to the title label. Tape it to the book front.

For pages, cut six 9½×12-inch pieces of kraft paper. Leaving a 1½-inch margin at the left side, use a computer to print out "Wedding Ghosts Guests" and irregular lines for guests to sign. Cross out the word "Ghosts" with a pen. Tear the right edge of each page. Use walnut ink and a paintbrush to splatter each page. Let dry.

Caution: Work over a sink filled with water; keep an old wet dishcloth nearby. Using a grill lighter or a lighted candle, burn the cut edges of the front and back covers and the kraft-paper pages. Work small sections at a time. The paper will smolder, so use the wet cloth to gently dab the edges as you work. When all the edges are burned, gently dab the ends again; watch carefully until all the pieces are completely cool.

Stack and tape the pages between the book front and back along the left edge, placing the fold of a folded tassel cord in between.

Nail-in-the-Coffin Party Favor *page 52*

MATERIALS

Tracing paper
Die-cut machine and box die cut (optional) (We used AccuCut Box 18.)
Dark gray card stock
Rub-on alphabet (We used Reminisce Font Buffet: Chicken King.)
Double-sided tape
Crafts glue
7-millimeter-diameter round red rhinestone
White chalk
⅔ yard of ½-inch-wide red ribbon

INSTRUCTIONS

Enlarge the box shape, *below,* to fit the card stock. Trace the shape on tracing paper; cut out. Trace the pattern on card stock and cut out the shape. If you're using a die cut, cut the shape with a die-cut machine.

Cut out the letters "R," "I," and "P" from the rub-on alphabet. Rub the letters on one side of the shape.

Fold the shape into a box, using double-sided tape to secure it at the side and bottom.

Glue a red rhinestone atop the dot on the "I." Rub all edges of the box with white chalk.

Fill the box with Halloween candy and tie it closed with ribbon.

Pen Holder *page 53*

MATERIALS

Black-and-white patterned papers (We used assorted items in the Formality Collection from One Heart…One Mind.)
2×2×2-inch wooden cube
Charcoal Colorbox Chalk Ink
Acrylic paints: black and white
1½-inch-diameter×1¾-inch-tall wooden spool
Crafts glue
Circle punches: ¼-inch and 1½-inch-diameter
Glue gun and hotmelt adhesive
Pen and 14-inch black quill feather

INSTRUCTIONS

From assorted patterned papers, cut two 2-inch squares and one 2×8¼-inch strip. Adhere the squares to the top and bottom of the cube; wrap and adhere the strip around the sides, slightly overlapping the ends. Ink all edges.

Paint the circumference of the spool white and the upper and lower edges of the spool black.

Cut a 6-inch length of patterned paper the width of the center of your spool. *Note:* If your spool has a curved middle, make tiny cuts (about ¹⁄₁₆ inch apart and ⅛ inch long) all along the top and the bottom long edge. Wrap and adhere the paper around the center of the spool, slightly overlapping the ends.

Punch one circle from a medallion-patterned paper. Punch a ¼-inch circle in the center. Ink the edges and adhere the paper to the top of the spool.

Hot-glue the spool to the top of the cube. Glue the feather to the pen and place it in the spool hole.

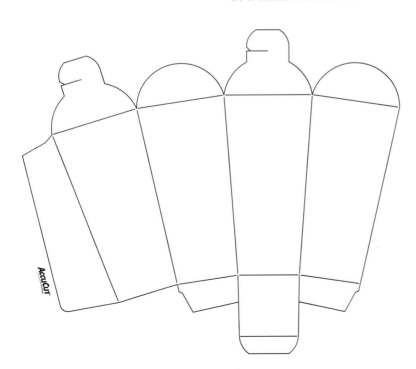

Oozing Brie

¾ of a 7- to 8-ounce jar oil-packed dried tomatoes
½ of a medium onion, sliced and separated into rings
4 teaspoons minced garlic
¼ cup slivered fresh basil leaves
⅛ teaspoon ground black pepper
2 15-ounce rounds of Brie with rind
1 tablespoon finely snipped fresh parsley or dried parsley, crushed
French bread slices cut ½ inch thick

Drain oil from dried tomatoes, reserving 3 tablespoons. Chop enough tomatoes for ½ cup.

In a large skillet, cook onion in 2 tablespoons reserved oil over medium heat until tender. Stir in garlic; cook and stir for 1 minute. Add chopped tomatoes and basil; cook and stir for 2 minutes. Remove from heat; stir in pepper.

Line a baking sheet with foil; place Brie on foil. Brush Brie with the remaining 1 tablespoon oil; sprinkle with parsley. Spread tomato mixture over tops. Cover and chill for 30 minutes or up to 5 hours.

Preheat oven to 350°F. Arrange bread slices on a baking sheet. Bake about 10 minutes or until lightly browned and toasted, turning once.

Bake Brie on center rack for 12 to 15 minutes or just until edges melt. Transfer Brie to a serving plate. Serve with toasted bread slices. Makes 20 servings.

Tipsy Tombstones

2 cups diced cooked chicken
1 cup diced celery (2 stalks)
½ cup diced green apple
3 slices bacon, crisp cooked and crumbled
½ cup dairy sour cream
1 cup mayonnaise or salad dressing
2 tablespoons lemon juice
Salt and freshly ground black pepper
28 slices firm whole wheat and/or rye bread, trimmed into tombstone shapes
1 8-ounce container whipped cream cheese
Finely chopped toasted pecans
Purple kale

In a large bowl, combine chicken, celery, apple, and bacon.

In a medium bowl, stir together sour cream, mayonnaise, and lemon juice. Add to chicken mixture; stir to coat. Season to taste with salt and pepper. Cover and chill for 2 to 24 hours.

To make tombstone sandwiches, spread chicken salad on half of the bread tombstones. Top with the remaining bread tombstones. Spread the edges of sandwiches with cream cheese. Coat cream cheese with chopped pecans. Use cream cheese to stick tombstones to plate. Add purple kale for ground cover. Makes 14 tombstones.

Walnut-Feta Yogurt Dip

4 cups plain low-fat or fat-free yogurt*
½ cup crumbled feta cheese (2 ounces)
⅓ cup chopped walnuts or pine nuts, toasted
2 tablespoons snipped dried tomatoes (not oil-packed)
2 teaspoons snipped fresh oregano or marjoram or 1 teaspoon dried oregano or marjoram, crushed
¼ teaspoon salt
⅛ teaspoon freshly ground black pepper
Walnut half and/or dried tomatoes (optional)
Assorted vegetable dippers

For yogurt cheese, line a yogurt strainer, sieve, or small colander with three layers of 100-percent–cotton cheesecloth or a clean paper coffee filter. Suspend lined strainer over a bowl. Spoon yogurt into strainer. Cover with plastic wrap. Chill for at least 24 hours or for up to 48 hours. Remove from refrigerator. Discard liquid in bowl.

Transfer yogurt cheese to a medium bowl. Stir in feta cheese, the chopped walnuts or pine nuts, 2 tablespoons dried tomatoes, oregano or marjoram, salt, and pepper. Cover and chill for at least 1 hour or for up to 24 hours. If desired, garnish with walnut half and/or additional tomatoes. Serve with vegetable dippers. Makes 2 cups.

*Note: Use yogurt that contains no gums, gelatin, or fillers. These ingredients may prevent the curd and whey from separating to make the yogurt cheese.

Body Bits Dip

8 ounces bulk pork sausage
1 medium red onion, sliced
1 5.3-ounce package cocktail wieners, halved crosswise
2 10-ounce cans diced tomatoes and green chilies, undrained
2 pounds American cheese, cubed
Assorted dippers

In a medium saucepan, cook sausage and onion over medium heat until sausage is no longer pink; drain. Transfer sausage mixture to a 3½- to 4-quart slow cooker. Stir in wieners, undrained tomatoes, and cheese. Cover and cook on high-heat setting for 1 to 2 hours or until cheese melts, stirring after 1 hour. To serve, keep warm on low setting, stirring occasionally. Serve with assorted dippers. Makes about 20 servings.

Pita Chips with Red Pepper Dip

- 1 24-ounce jar roasted red sweet peppers with garlic, drained
- 1 6-ounce can tomato paste
- 1 tablespoon snipped fresh thyme
- 2 teaspoons sugar
- ⅛ teaspoon cayenne pepper
  Fresh thyme sprig
  Assorted dippers

Place drained peppers and tomato paste in a blender or food-processor bowl. Cover and blend or process until nearly smooth. Transfer mixture to a serving bowl. Stir in snipped thyme, sugar, and pepper. Garnish with thyme sprig. Makes ½ cup.

Eyeball Punch

  Canned litchis, drained
  Maraschino cherries without stems
  Dark red punch or fruit drink, chilled

Cut a slit in each litchi. Stuff a maraschino cherry into each fruit so it resembles an eye. Place stuffed litchis on a large baking pan. Freeze until solid.

To serve, pour punch into a large bowl. Add the litchis.

Bloody-Rimmed Martinis

  Red decorating icing writing gel
- ¾ cup half-and-half or light cream
- ½ cup coconut-flavored rum
- ¼ cup vanilla vodka or vodka
- ¼ cup cream of coconut
  Ice cubes

Carefully pipe red gel around the rim of four to six martini glasses, letting it drip down the sides. Set aside.

In a pitcher, stir together the half-and-half, coconut rum, vodka, and cream of coconut. Place ice cubes in a martini shaker. Add coconut mixture. Cover and shake. Divide mixture among prepared martini glasses. Makes 4 to 6 drinks.

Graveyard Gravel

- 3 cups semisweet chocolate pieces
- 1 14-ounce can sweetened condensed milk
- 2 tablespoons butter
- 1½ teaspoons vanilla
  Dash salt
- 2 cups tiny marshmallows
  Unsweetened cocoa powder mixed with an equal amount of powdered sugar

Line a 9×9×2- or an 8×8×2-inch baking pan with foil; set aside.

In a medium saucepan, heat and stir chocolate pieces, condensed milk, butter, vanilla, and salt over medium heat until melted and smooth. Remove from heat; stir in marshmallows just until combined. Spread mixture evenly in the foil-lined pan. Using a table knife or thin metal spatula, swirl marshmallows through fudge in pan until marshmallows are mostly melted. Cover and chill about 2 hours or until firm.

Using a small scoop, scoop fudge and shape into rocks (fudge will be sticky). Roll in cocoa mixture. Makes about 80 pieces.

Minty Stones

- 2 3-ounce packages cream cheese, softened
- 1 teaspoon peppermint extract
- 6 cups powdered sugar
- 2 tablespoons purchased black icing
  Black sanding or decorating sugar (optional)

In a medium bowl, stir together softened cream cheese and peppermint extract. Gradually add powdered sugar, stirring until mixture is smooth. (Knead in the last of the powdered sugar with your hands.) Add black icing; knead until food coloring is evenly distributed.

Form cream-cheese mixture into ¾-inch balls. Roll each ball in sanding sugar if desired; place on waxed paper. Cover mints with paper towels; let dry overnight. Store in a tightly covered container in the refrigerator or freeze up to 1 month. Makes 96 to 120 pieces.

Family-Style
Fright Night

Boring family party? Nevermore!
Our supereasy recipes (trust us—they're as easy as
opening a few jars and boxes!) will please picky
party guests of all ages.

DESIGNED BY LORI HELLANDER   PHOTOGRAPHED BY GREG SCHEIDEMANN   WRITTEN BY ANN MCCURDY YOUNG   FOOD PRODUCED BY LAURA COLLINS

Halloween Fixin's

Start your party by setting out munchies with descriptive signs to make everyone chuckle. Your s'mores, that old campfire treat, will get rave reviews for dessert at this Halloween shindig. Psst ... a nice take-home gift for the adults is a rolled-up copy of all the recipes.

Spiderweb Soup

Giving everyday tomato soup a ghoulish makeover can happen in a snap. Squeeze on a mixture of sour cream and milk in a spiral shape over the soup; use a toothpick to drag lines from the center out toward the edges. Voila—you're ready to catch a fly!

Out on a Limb

Fun bags full of treats will help keep little guests from getting spooked by the sight of bats and ghosts hanging in tree branches.

Yummy Mummy Dogs

Fill up hungry tummies with Mummy Dogs, a smile-inducing finger food. Refrigerated breadstick dough makes this crowd-pleaser a cinch to make. For eyes, press capers into the dough before baking.

A Few Feathered Friends
Give your guests something to crow about by perching a few crows (available in crafts stores) in strategic locations for the evening.

Chicken Feed
All ghosts and goblins will love digging into this granola concoction. Prepare this mixture of seeds, nuts, oats, and a healthy dose of sweet ingredients several days before the event.

For recipes and instructions, see page 67.

Where else but on a Halloween tabletop will you find spiderweb soup, mummy dogs, and granola chicken feed!

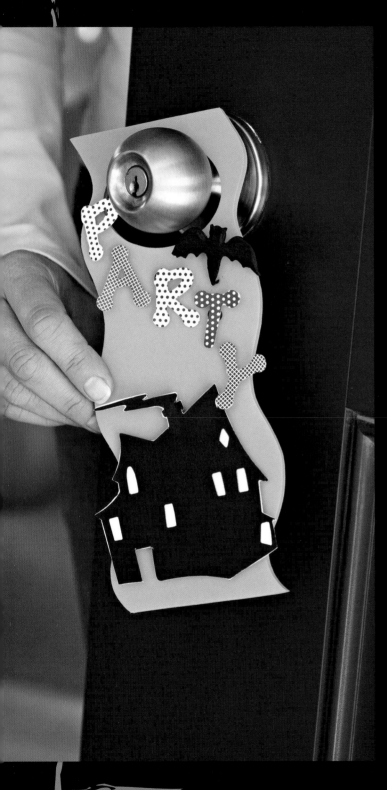

Party Invitation

MATERIALS

Computer and printer
White letter-size computer printer paper
Crafts glue
Precut green crafts-foam doorknob hanger
Die-cut letters to spell the word Party
Black crafts foam
Paper punch
Small bat shape

INSTRUCTIONS

In a word-processing or page layout program, print a clip-art haunted house silhouette in a size to fit on the doorknob hanger. Print out the desired number of copies and cut out the shapes. Print out the text for the invitation in a size that fits the hanger. Use white crafts glue to adhere the text block to the back of the hanger.

To give dimension to the haunted house and lettering on the front of the invitation, punch eight to 10 dots from black crafts foam and glue to the back of the letters and the haunted house. Then glue the letters, the house, and the bat to the doorknob hanger.

Food Signs

MATERIALS

For each sign:
Shadow-box scrapbook paper
Rub-on and die-cut letters
Crafts glue
Black drinking straw
Transparent tape

INSTRUCTIONS

Tear the desired shape from the shadow-box paper. Use a combination of rub-on and die-cut letters to spell the words you want. Adhere the rub-on letters following the manufacturer's instructions and using crafts glue to apply the die-cut letters to the shadow-box paper.

Cut a 3-inch-long piece of drinking straw; cut a 1½-inch-long slit in the piece. Slide the sign into the slit and secure at the back with tape.

Treat Bags

MATERIALS

Small paper bags: white and black
Deckle-edge scissors
Tracing paper
White sparkle felt
Black crafts foam
Paper punch
Scraps of paper: black and green
Black hanging ribbon
Crafts glue

INSTRUCTIONS

Cut around the top of each bag with the deckle-edge scissors. Referring to the photo on *page 64,* sketch the ghost and bat outlines onto tracing paper; cut out. Trace the ghost pattern onto the felt and the bat pattern onto the crafts foam. Trace around the shapes, and cut them out.

Punch out circles from the black and green paper. Glue the eyes to the ghost and the bat. Glue the ghost onto the black bag and the bat onto the white bag. Punch out circles on the bag for the hanging ribbon. Thread the ribbon through the holes, and knot the ends.

Super-Easy S'Mores

8 chocolate or regular graham cracker squares
3 tablespoons chocolate-hazelnut spread
3 tablespoons marshmallow creme

Place graham cracker squares on a work surface; spread 4 squares with chocolate-hazelnut spread. Spread remaining graham cracker squares with marshmallow creme. Place graham crackers, marshmallow sides down, on top of chocolate-hazelnut spread. Place on a microwave-safe plate.

Microwave, uncovered, on 100% power (high) for 30 seconds. (If you want to heat the s'mores one or two at a time, microwave one s'more on 100% power [high] for 10 seconds or two s'mores for 20 seconds.) Serve at once. Makes 4 s'mores.

Peanut Butter S'Mores: Prepare as directed, except use chocolate graham cracker squares and substitute peanut butter for the chocolate-hazelnut spread.

Make-Ahead Tip: Prepare up to 30 minutes ahead. Microwave just before serving.

MUMMY
DOGS

Oh Mummy!
Kids won't need encouragement to eat a hot dog, so be sure to fix plenty of these Mummy Dogs. They'll want seconds just for the fun of dipping them into the different condiment bowls.

Mummy Dogs

1 11-ounce package refrigerated breadsticks (12 breadsticks)
12 jumbo frankfurters
Catsup and mustard
Capers

Preheat oven to 375°F. Unwrap breadsticks. Stretch each breadstick to 12 inches. Wrap dough around frankfurters, letting the frankfurters show slightly through the bread. Press in capers for eyes. Bake in preheated oven for about 12 minutes or until bread is golden brown. Serve with catsup and mustard. Makes 12 snacks.

Chicken Feed

¼ cup apple jelly or desired-flavor jelly
3 tablespoons sugar
2 tablespoons butter or margarine
½ teaspoon ground cinnamon
1 cup rolled oats
½ cup peanuts or slivered almonds
¼ cup shelled sunflower seeds
¼ cup coconut
1 cup candy-coated peanuts

Preheat oven to 325°F. Place jelly, sugar, butter or margarine, and cinnamon in a medium saucepan. Cook and stir over low heat until butter is melted and sugar dissolved. Stir in the oats, peanuts or almonds, sunflower seeds, and coconut until combined.

Pour the mixture into an ungreased baking pan. Spread the mixture in an even layer. Bake for 20 to 25 minutes or until lightly browned, stirring once or twice.

Transfer mixture to a large piece of foil to cool. Store in a covered container in a cool, dry place up to 2 weeks. Just before serving, stir in candy-coated peanuts. Makes 5 cups.

Weave an Easy Web

(a) Prepare a mixture of 3 tablespoons of sour cream and 1 tablespoon of milk. Fill a plastic condiment bottle with the mixture. Carefully squeeze several circles on the surface of warm soup. (b) Use a wood skewer to drag lines from the center out toward the edges to create a web design.

pumpkin-patch party

Jack-o'-lanterns grin from ear to ear—it's pumpkin time, didn't you hear?

WRITTEN BY HEIDI PALKOVIC PHOTOGRAPHED BY GREG SCHEIDEMANN

While haunting ghouls, bone-chilling skeletons, and shadowy figures are all part of the fun at Halloween, good old-fashioned jack-o'-lanterns rule at this Halloween bash—giving it a merry theme that children of all ages will enjoy. The best part? Everything at this party is created using modest, store-bought materials along with a few perennial Halloween favorites—all you have to do is give them a creative twist.

To take the fright out of party planning, divide the room into three stations: a serving table for treats, a drink cart for refreshments, and a crafts area for creating pumpkin-theme projects. Near the door, place a trunk filled with Halloween-costume accessories where kids can don their favorites for a quick dress-up idea upon entering the party. Your guests will soon be grinning as big as ol' Jack himself.

Tower of Treats
The smiling fellows atop these frosted cupcakes, *opposite left*, are really suckers made with candy melts and a mold. After you've painted the details, poke the suckers into cupcakes baked right inside colorful latex cake cups.

Ghoulish Goodies
Transform orange and black paper drink cups, *opposite right*, into frightfully fun take-home treat containers. "Carve" the design into the side of one cup, nest a contrasting cup inside, and tie on a name tag for each guest.

Jack-on-a-Stick
Dress up store-bought sugar cookies, *this page*, with whimsical jack-o'-lantern faces cut from rolled-out orange gumdrop candy. Sandwich a layer of chocolate frosting between two cookies, and then add a mini paint stick for a handle.

Goodies, crafts, and treats galore will keep boys and girls begging for more.

Party Like a Pumpkin

Set a scene that's merry, not scary. For an inexpensive yet clever table, use steel garbage cans as legs for a plywood tabletop covered with rickrack-trimmed burlap. A dish drainer makes a handy holder for orange plates fitted with craft-foam stems and chenille vines.

What's Brewing?
Set up a drink station in the corner of a room where kids can mix and mingle while partaking of their favorite beverages, *opposite left.* Transform a plastic pumpkin into a spiderlike ice bucket with chenille stems.

Gather the Ghouls
Give a hint to all the bewitching party fun to come with an easy-to-make pumpkin invite, *opposite right.*

Costume Cuties
Parents will welcome this stress-free costume idea: Fill a trunk with costume bits and pieces, such as cowboy hats, bunny ears, fairy wings, and pirate eye patches, *above,* so kids can dress up when they arrive.

Ghostly Delights
Tissue-paper circles embellished with punched shapes turn store-bought suckers into merry jack-o'-lanterns, *above right.* An upside-down glass covered with cheesecloth gives a ghostly effect.

Say Cheese
Kids will devour these open-face bologna-and-cheese sandwiches, *right,* that are a cinch to make using small cookie cutters to create the cheese faces. A basil leaf and bread-crust stem complete the pumpkin package.

Giggles, smiles, and fun await at a pumpkin party that's easy

Pick a Pumpkin
Ready, set, toss! This pumpkin toss game, *left,* is sure to score big with party guests. Setup couldn't be simpler—just cut out the pumpkins from poster board and attach them to the side of a cardboard box.

Having a Ball
Turn gold table-tennis balls into mini pumpkins, *above left and right.* Get them ready for game action by drawing pumpkin faces with permanent marker onto the sides.

Shake 'em Up
What would a celebration be without the merry clatter of noisemakers? Kids can make these pumpkin-face shakers, *opposite top left,* by lacing two plates together and adding dry beans and jingle bells for a happy sound.

Magnetic Makeover
Who knew a plain lunch box could be so cute? Prep silver lunch boxes by painting them orange, and then give kids painted wooden shapes and self-adhesive magnets so they can create their own ghoulish pumpkin grins, *opposite top right* and *bottom.*

to create. Silly faces everywhere hint that fun is in the air.

PRODUCED BY KARIN LIDBECK BRENT, HOLLY RAIBIKIS,
LAURA HOLTORF COLLINS, AND ELAINE KOONCE

Pumpkin Garland

MATERIALS

Card stock: orange and black
Black permanent marking pen
Double-stick tape
11 binder clips
Twine

INSTRUCTIONS

Draw and cut out 11 stemmed pumpkins from orange card stock. Cut letters from black card stock.

Accordion-fold the pumpkins with approximately 1 inch between each fold. Fill in the stem area with the black marker. Tape a letter to each folded pumpkin, being careful not to flatten the folds.

String a length of twine along a wall or above a doorway. Attach each pumpkin to the twine with a binder clip.

Party Invitation

MATERIALS

Card stock: orange and black (optional)
Black permanent marker (optional)
½- to 1-inch-tall black sticker letters

INSTRUCTIONS

Enlarge the pattern at *right* to the size you want. Place the stem on the fold of a folded piece of orange card stock and cut out the shape. Draw the eyes, nose, and stem with black permanent marker onto one pumpkin side as indicated, or cut out the shapes from black card stock and glue them to the pumpkin. Use a crafts knife to cut out the mouth on the front pumpkin only.

With the invitation closed, position sticker letters inside the mouth to spell out a party message.

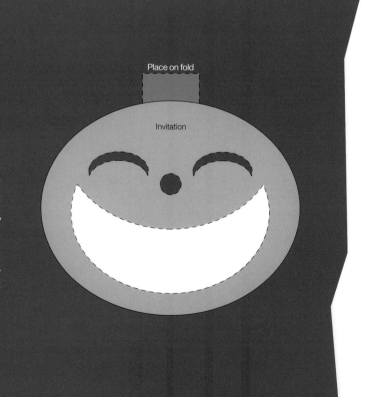

Place on fold

Invitation

Ghoul Favor Cups

MATERIALS

- Orange and black paper drink cups
- Orange card stock
- Orange chenille stems
- Glass beads
- Crafts knife
- Small drinking glass to fit inside paper cup

INSTRUCTIONS

Referring to the photograph, on *page 72,* pencil a face design on a cup, or trace the sample pattern, *below.*

Insert a small drinking glass inside a traced paper drink cup. Using a crafts knife, carefully cut out the pattern along the lines, using the glass as support so the paper cup does not bend out of shape while you're cutting. Remove the glass.

Trim approximately 1 inch off the top of each cup with decorative-edge scissors, or use straight scissors to cut a design to give the ghoul a hairline. Insert an uncut contrasting cup inside the cut cup.

Punch a single hole on opposite sides of the inner cup. Print the recipient's name onto orange card stock and cut it out. Punch a hole into one end of the name strip. Cut a 10-inch length of chenille stem and thread a bead onto each end. Thread the name strip onto the chenille stem and wrap the ends through the holes of the inner cup for a handle.

Pumpkin Thermos Drinks

MATERIALS

- Crafts foam: green, black, and orange
- Press-on letters
- Crafts glue

INSTRUCTIONS

Referring to the photograph, draw various pumpkin shapes on orange foam and cut out. If desired, cut stems from contrasting colors and apply with glue. Cut a band of foam, and glue it to the back of each pumpkin. Apply letters of your choice. Wrap the bands around your thermoses and glue the ends together.

Bat Bowl

MATERIALS

- Black crafts foam
- Plastic pumpkin bucket
- Crafts knife
- Tape

INSTRUCTIONS

Enlarge the wing pattern, *below,* to the size you want. Trace two wing patterns onto black crafts foam; cut out the pieces. With the crafts knife, carefully cut a slit on each side of the bucket. Insert the bat wings and secure them with tape on the inside of the bucket.

Pumpkin Noisemakers

MATERIALS

½×12-inch dowel

Black acrylic paint

Green crafts foam

Orange disposable plates

Black permanent marking pen

Hole punch

Dry beans and small jingle bells

Yarn: green or black

Glue gun and hotmelt adhesive (optional)

INSTRUCTIONS

Paint the dowel black; let dry.

Using a photocopier, enlarge the patterns, *below,* to the size you want. Trace the patterns onto the green crafts foam, and cut out. Cut slits in the center of the leaves as indicated on the pattern.

Using the photograph as a guide, draw a face onto the flat side of one plate with a black permanent marking pen; let dry.

Hold the face plate and a plain plate with rims together. Using a hole punch, evenly space holes around the rims through both plates. Place a few dry beans and a few jingle bells in the gap between the plates and lay the dowel through the center of the plates, allowing a short end to stick out the top for a pumpkin stem and a large amount to stick out the bottom for a handle. Lace yarn through the holes to hold the two plates together. Place the leaves on the dowel through the slits and hot-glue in place.

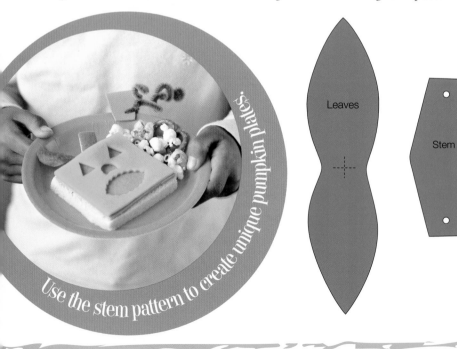

Use the stem pattern to create unique pumpkin plates.

Leaves

Stem

Pumpkin Lunch Box

MATERIALS

Round metal lunch box with handle

Orange spray paint

Assorted unfinished wood shapes: circles, stars, and hearts

Acrylic paint: red, orange, yellow, and black

Self-adhesive magnets

Scrabble pieces

INSTRUCTIONS

In a well-ventilated area, spray-paint the lunch box orange; let dry.

Divide unfinished wood shapes into four assorted groupings. Paint each group with one color of acrylic paint; let dry.

To ease assembly, place the colored wood shapes, the Scrabble pieces, and the self-adhesive magnets each in a small container. Have kids peel off the paper backings from the magnets and adhere magnets to backs of desired shapes and decorations. Arrange magnetic shapes on lid of lunch box as desired.

Pumpkin Toss Game

MATERIALS

Poster board: orange and black
Cardboard box
Spray adhesive
Crafts knife
8 to 10 orange table-tennis balls
Medium-tip black permanent
    marking pen

INSTRUCTIONS

Using a photocopier, enlarge the patterns as indicated on the pattern. Trace the pumpkin patterns onto orange poster board and the eye and nose patterns onto black poster board; cut out the pieces, but do not cut out the pumpkin mouth openings yet.

Tape one end of the box shut and cut off the flaps on the opposite side. Place the box with the open-side down and use spray adhesive to attach the black poster board to the front of the box. Beginning with the largest pumpkin, use spray adhesive to attach it along the bottom edge of the poster board. Spacing the pumpkins about 1 inch apart, adhere the medium pumpkin above the large pumpkin and the small pumpkin on top.

Cut out the pumpkin mouths through all the layers using a crafts knife.

Referring to the photograph on *page 74*, draw pumpkin faces on table-tennis balls using a medium-tip black permanent marking pen. Allow the faces to dry.

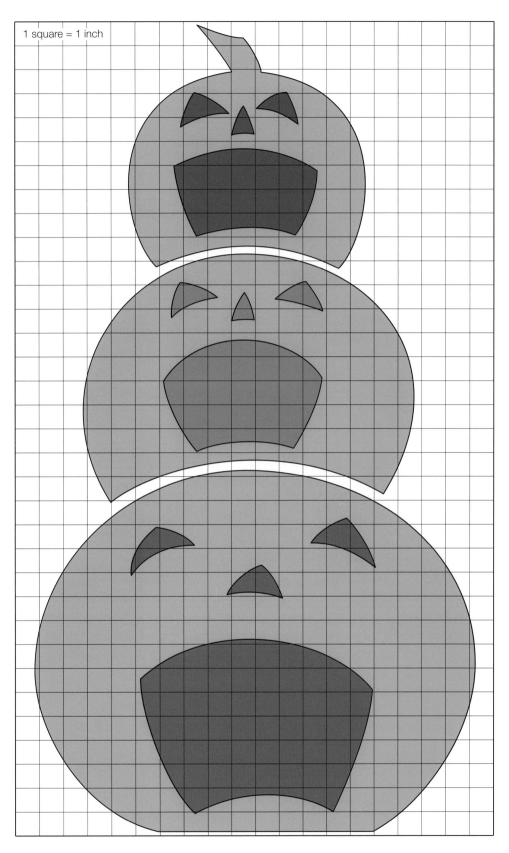

1 square = 1 inch

The bewitching hour has finally arrived and it's time to throw a terror-ific party for your little ghosts and goblins. Our ghoul-proof guide to throwing a spooktacular party is packed with frighteningly fun ideas for your Halloween festivities.

ultimate PARTY GUIDE

WRITTEN BY BECKY MOLLENKAMP

BOO-dacious
Halloween BASH
date:
October 31, 2007
time:
6:00 to midnite
where:
the Sanders'
HAUNTED HOUSE
Costume required!!!

Invitations

Catch the spirit of Halloween fun and invite your friends over for a spooktacular time. After setting the date and developing a guest list, send invites two to three weeks prior to the event. If you asked guests to RSVP, call anyone who has not responded two to three days before the party.

watchful eyes

Bright eyes and spiders boo-tify this skeleton wreath. The make-it-in-minutes project is simply a store-bought twig wreath embellished with modeling-clay eyes and a tin banner that dares guests to enter. For a spookier welcome, sculpt the eyes using glow-in-the-dark clay.

wicked welcome

Set the mood for a fun evening of Halloween revelry with an invitation that's just as appealing, *above*. Peeking from a hole in the front of the card, a pom-pom spider adds fuzzy dimension. When the invitation is opened, the spider stays put on the second page, where all of the party details are listed.

ghoulish greetings

Halloween should be fun and quirky—and so should your party. Dare guests to come with a whimsical invite crafted simply from layers of card stock, *opposite*. Featuring bold colors and fancy ribbon trim, the card is sure to entice your fellow spooks to join the fun.

You may think it goes without saying that a Halloween party is a costumed event, but your guests may not. Let them know your expectations in the invitation.

decorations

Deck the halls with pumpkins, ghosts, and felt-embellished accents to set a mood that's devilishly delightful. You'll find all the supplies you need for these creepy-crawly designs at a crafts store. Allow plenty of time before the party to craft the decorations and be sure to get the children involved in the process.

PARTY TIME LINE

Party day will be here before you can say "Boo." Reduce stress by following this simple checklist.

ONE WEEK PRIOR

✔ Make or purchase the party favors, prizes, and decorations, including the piñata.
✔ Assemble materials for the crafts projects.
✔ Buy nonperishable groceries.

THREE DAYS BEFORE

✔ Double-check the final guest list.
✔ Make a schedule for what you'll do at the party.

DAY BEFORE

✔ Lay down newspapers or a disposable tablecloth for crafts projects.
✔ Purchase perishable foods.
✔ Prepare foods that can be made in advance.
✔ Put up decorations.

it's a wrap

This menacing mummy pumpkin will wrap guests in fear with his piercing black eyes. Cut slits into a white or painted pumpkin, including two for the eyes. Glue a marble into each eye opening.

super spooks

These playful pranksters will leave you cackling with delight. The fiendish duo starts with spray-painted gourds, which are trimmed with accents of crafts foam, wire, and features made using a black marker. If the gourds roll, poke pins into the bottoms to steady them.

seeing silverware

Keep an eye on party guests with this spooky silverware. Cover inexpensive utensils with black polymer clay and top with plastic doll eyes. Bake the decorated silverware according to clay package directions. Carefully hand-wash silverware after use.

run amok

Evoke screams of delight with this playful table runner. The no-sew project is easy to concoct using felt and glue. Attach black felt silhouettes to the orange runner, and finish the edges by gluing rickrack along the sides. In just a few minutes, you can set the scene for a feast of Halloween treats.

MOOD MUSIC

Jazz up your party by blasting some scary songs. Search music stores or online for compilation CDs featuring spooky tunes, or create your own play-list with these mysterious melodies.

"Boris the Spider"

"THRILLER"

"Somebody's Watching Me"

"TWILIGHT ZONE"

"Witch Doctor"

hang loose

Set a ghostly party theme with simple handmade cutouts like this door hanger. Trace a ghost shape onto white card stock; cut it out. Carve a hole in the center for a doorknob and add eyes and a message with marker (or print them onto the card stock before cutting out the design).

Boo!

FRIGHTENING LIGHTS

To bring the eerie mood of Halloween night inside, replace the lightbulbs around your house with colored ones. Orange or yellow lights cast a spooky glow, while black lights are extra creepy. Find the bulbs in a home center or party store.

drinks & snacks

Children love their food to look gross but taste great. These creative concoctions are fit for ghouls and boys of all ages. There's no need to serve an elaborate meal; simply choose a handful of snack foods that scream Halloween. If possible, prepare the food ahead of time to reduce party-day stress.

slimy sipper

Brew up some fun—and a giggle or two—with this gooey blue brew. The "slime" is blueberry-flavored gelatin floating in lemonade and lemon-lime soda. To make sure the slime for Blue Slime is the right consistency, avoid setting the gelatin completely. Chill the gelatin in the refrigerator only until it is softly set. It should not hold a cut edge when you spoon into it.

vegetable delight

Add a healthy snack to the menu with fresh veggies arranged in a cute, kid-friendly cat face. To turn the deviled-egg filling a creepy green, add blue food coloring to the mixture.

For party fun on Halloween night, consider giving out prizes for silliest, scariest, and most creative costumes.

smart cookies

Perform a little magic on refrigerated cookie dough to create cutout cookies. Shape refrigerated dough into bats, rats, cats, or witches, and then bake and decorate with frosting and candy.

Scary Cookie Critters

1   18-ounce roll refrigerated sugar or peanut butter cookie dough
1   16-ounce can vanilla frosting
    Paste food coloring
    Decorating gel
    Large and small gumdrops
    Small decorative candies
    Coarse sugar
    String licorice

Freeze dough for at least 2 hours. Meanwhile, divide frosting among four bowls; tint with paste food coloring as desired. Cover and set aside. Preheat oven to 350°F. Cut dough into ¼-inch slices. Shape desired critters (see *below left*). Place shapes about 2 inches apart on ungreased cookie sheet. Bake for 7 to 9 minutes or until edges are lightly browned. Cool on wire rack. Decorate as desired.

For Bats: Make jagged cut through center of each slice; separate pieces. Bake and cool as directed. Decorate with frosting and gel. Add small gumdrop halves for ears and small candies for eyes. Sprinkle with sugar.

For Rats and Cats: Make jagged M-shape cut through center of each slice; separate pieces. (Pieces with three points form rats and pieces with two points form cats.) Bake and cool as directed. Decorate with frosting. For each rat, add licorice for tail, small candy for eye, and large gumdrop slice for ear. For each cat, decorate face with small candies.

For Witches: Make jagged cut through center of each slice. Pull cut pieces apart slightly to form open mouth. Bake and cool as directed. Decorate with frosting and gel. For each witch, cut hat out of rolled-out large gumdrop; press onto head. Add small candies for eye and warts.

weird science

PLAY WITH YOUR FOOD

Turn your kitchen into a mad scientist's laboratory for a fun party game. Place grapes (eyeballs), banana peels (tongues), gummy worms, and other creepy-feeling items in boxes. Blindfold the kids and have them guess what they are feeling.

monster mouths

These edible monster mouths will get party guests talking. They are so easy to make that you can whip up a plateful of apple-peanut-butter-candy-corn mouths in just minutes. One apple makes four mouths.

activities & favors

A Halloween party isn't complete without fun games and activities to keep the kids busy and entertained. To keep your event moving, choose four to six activities and games for the day (if your child is school-age, consider selecting these together).

treats incognito

Give partygoers something extra to enjoy by letting them put together this sweet masterpiece. Frankenstein is made by gluing together boxed and wrapped candy, packs of gum, and fruit chews. His friend, Mr. Bones, is a lollipop wrapped in tissue paper with chenille-stem arms, legs, and body.

terrific trimmings

Keep little witches and goblins entertained with this frightfully fun project. Even young children can craft these easy-to-make ornaments, which require only felt and glue. When the designs are finished, fill the pouches with small candies. By Suzonne Stirling for Perfect Glue from Liquid Nails Brand Construction Adhesives; 866/321-4583; www.perfectglue.com.

game time

Hosting a Halloween party can be easier than you think, as long as you have plenty of activities to keep the kids busy. If your creative well runs dry after bobbing for apples and a costume contest, get more ideas at bhg.com/halloweengames.

in the bag

Give your party a spirited "boo-dacious" theme with a take-home favor box and bag made from embellishments from the scrapbooking aisle of the crafts store. Add paper, ribbon, and squiggly eyes to give oomph to a white card-stock die-cut box, *right*. Fill a clear plastic bag with treats and seal it with a topper made from scrapbooking paper and stickers, *below*.

Relax and enjoy the party. It's OK if things don't go as planned.

take a swing

Stage your own slasher movie as the kids take a stab at this pumpkin piñata. Made from a papier-mâché-covered balloon, the pumpkin hides a stash of treats behind its smile. Cover the design in colored paper and dress it up with paper stockings, lace-up paper shoes, and a glittery party hat.

SPINE-TINGLING STORY TIME

If your partygoers are mature enough, treat them to a haunted book reading. Look online for spooky tales or visit your local library for kid-friendly ghost stories, such as the *Scary Stories* series by Alvin Schwartz and Stephen Gammel.

Ghoulish Greetings

MATERIALS

Rumble Tumble sheets from One Heart
… One Mind: card-stock invites and
die-cut card-stock coveralls
Charcoal chalk ink
⅛-inch hole punch
Black-and-white sheer polka-dot
ribbon

DIRECTIONS

Cut along the green zigzag edge of the
coveralls sheet. With zigzag points at the
top, cut a 4×11-inch rectangle (it will be
four points wide). Fold down the border.
Add party information to the card-stock
invites sheet. Ink all paper edges using
chalk ink.

Insert invite under the folded border.
Punch two holes 1 inch apart in the
center of the border. Tie with ribbon.

Wicked Welcome

MATERIALS

Card stock: lime and black
Pinking shears
Lime stripe paper
Double-sided adhesive tape
Hole punch (the size of the pom-pom)
Thick crafts glue
Black pom-pom
Black adhesive letters
Black marking pen
Small circle template
2 wiggle eyes

DIRECTIONS

Referring to the photograph on *page
81*, make the card using card stock
and stripe paper. Punch a hole in the
lower half of the card front. Glue pom-
pom to corresponding spot on inside of
card. Add invitation information using
adhesive letters and marking pen. Use
the template to draw the web and to
write on a curve; draw legs with the pen.
Glue the eyes in place.

Frankenstein

MATERIALS

Candy: tiny box of raisins, M&M's
Minis candies (1 red, 2 green),
1 roll of Smarties, 4 Tootsie Flavor
Roll Twisties, 1 box of Nerds,
2 orange Starburst fruit chews,
2 5-stick packages chewing gum
Paper: green and purple
Double-sided adhesive tape
Permanent marking pen
Canned icing
Chenille stem

DIRECTIONS

Wrap the raisin box with green paper,
taping the paper in place. Use the black
marking pen to draw facial features. Use
icing to add an M&M's nose and two
neck bolts (two Smarties). For the arms,
use pieces of chenille stem to twist the
Twisties together at the elbows. Slip a
length of chenille stem through the top
of the box for the shoulders. Twist one
end of the shoulder stem around the
top of one arm. Trim and attach the
remaining arm. Cut away excess chenille
stem. Cut a vest from purple paper to fit
around the candy box. Tape the vest in

Watchful Eyes

MATERIALS

Sculpey modeling clay: orange, yellow, and black
Unpainted tin banner sign
Purple acrylic paint
Orange acrylic dimensional paint
Glue gun and hotmelt adhesive
10 black plastic spiders and spider webbing
Twig wreath

DIRECTIONS

Pull off small amounts of orange, yellow, and black modeling clay. Roll and
flatten small amounts of the orange and yellow clay into ovals. Roll and flatten
black clay into small circles. Attach the black clay pieces to the yellow and
orange clay pieces; then attach the eyes in pairs. Follow the clay manufacturer's
instructions to bake.

Base-coat the sign with purple acrylic paint. Write "Dare to Enter!" on the
sign using dimensional paint. Hot-glue the sign and eyes to the wreath. Drape
the webbing and plastic spiders on the twigs of the wreath.

place, and then use icing to add green Minis to the front for buttons. Hot-glue the fruit-chews feet to the front of the gum legs. Hot-glue the legs and the head to the body.

Mr. Bones

MATERIALS

Shiny white fabric tissue paper
Permanent black marking pen
Tootsie Roll Pop
Adhesive tape
3 thick white chenille stems

DIRECTIONS

Cut a 4¼-inch square from the fabric tissue paper. Draw a face with the marking pen. Wrap the tissue paper over the lollipop. Secure the gathers to the stick, wrapping them with a small piece of tape. For the rib cage, wrap the end of a chenille stem around the taped area. Locate the center of another chenille stem, and tightly wrap it around the neck. Bend the stem at the shoulders, elbows, and hands. To make the legs, shape the remaining chenille stem into two legs, twisting the center of the legs around the base of the sucker stick.

Run Amok

MATERIALS

Orange felt (long enough to cover table with 12-inch overhang on each side)
Black rickrack (approximately 9 yards for a 6-foot table)
Adhesive (We used Perfect Glue 1.)
Halloween silhouette images
Black felt

DIRECTIONS

Cut orange felt 16 inches wide by the length of your table plus 24 inches. Glue rickrack onto runner to define sections, allowing 12 inches on each end and dividing other sections equally.

Referring to the photograph, draw silhouettes onto back side of black felt; cut out. Use adhesive to attach the shapes and rickrack to the runner.

In the Bag

MATERIALS

4½×8½-inch clear plastic bag
Rumble Tumble die-cut card stock coveralls from One Heart … One Mind
Charcoal chalk ink
4 wiggle eyes
Card stock: white
Double-sided adhesive tape

DIRECTIONS

Fill bag with goodies and seal closed.

For the topper, cut along the green zigzag edge of the coveralls sheet. Cut the sheet ½ inch wider than the bag opening and 5 inches long (including the zigzag border). Fold shape in half so the back straight edge is just above the zigzag border. Ink edges using the chalk ink. Glue wiggle eyes to points on border.

Print "Boo-dacious Treats!" on white card stock. Tear around the edges, ink with chalk ink, and tape to the topper. Tape topper in place.

Terrific Trimmings

MATERIALS

Wool felt in assorted colors
Adhesive (We used Perfect Glue 1.)
Fine-tip paintbrush
Mini hole punch
Thin ribbon

DIRECTIONS

Draw simple Halloween-shape silhouettes onto wool felt; cut out two for each ornament. Glue silhouettes together by applying a thin line of adhesive with a paintbrush around the edges, leaving the top edge open to create a pocket for filling with candy. Cut features for each shape out of felt, and glue to surface of ornaments. Punch a hole in each side of ornament and thread a piece of ribbon through, knotting behind the ornament.

Favor Box

MATERIALS

9×5×2-inch white card-stock basket
  (We used a die-cut from AccuCut.)
Rumble Tumble sheets from One Heart
  …One Mind: card-stock invites
Patterned paper: green-and-white grid
Mini pinking sheers
Charcoal chalk ink
Black fine-tip permanent marking
  pen
Double-sided adhesive tape
Circle punches: 1½, ⅞, and ¾ inch
Wiggle eyes: 2 large and 2 small
Adhesive-foam pieces
Assorted Halloween stickers
Orange tissue paper and treats
Assorted ribbons

DIRECTIONS

Referring to the photo on *page 87*, cut the basket sides from the card-stock invites and patterned paper, trimming some of the edges with pinking sheers if desired. Ink the edges with the charcoal chalk ink. Add stitching lines with the marking pen. Tape the papers to the basket.

Using the 1½-inch punch, punch two circles from card-stock invites for the large eyes. With the ¾-inch punch, punch a circle from a dark purple area of the polka-dot sheet for a nose. Ink all the pieces with chalk ink. Tape eyelash fiber and wiggle eyes to the large circles. Secure eyes and nose to the basket with adhesive foam pieces.

Print "Boo-dacious" on a 1½×4½-inch piece of white card stock. Tear the edges, ink them with chalk ink, and then tape in place. Add "Happy" and "Halloween" stickers.

Make smaller versions of the eyes using card-stock invites, the ⅞-inch punch, and small google eyes. Tape the eyes to the basket.

Fill the basket with orange tissue paper and treats; tie the handles together with assorted ribbons.

Arm for Short Gourd

Arm for Tall Gourd

Bat

Hat Brim

Pumpkin

Super Spooks

MATERIALS

Small pear-shape gourds
White spray primer
Paper punch
Crafts foam: white, black, orange, and
  yellow
White map pins
Black fine-tip permanent marking pen
Crafts glue
Acrylic paints: black and white
Colored wire: orange and purple

DIRECTIONS

In a well-ventilated work area, spray-paint the gourds white. Let dry.

To make the eyes, punch out black circles from black foam. Attach the black circles to the gourds using white map pins. Use a black marking pen to draw mouths and make a dot for each nose.

Trace the patterns and cut out. Trace around the patterns on craft foam and cut out. Glue the details on the pumpkin shape. To make eyes on the bat, dip the handle of a paintbrush into white paint and dot onto the foam. When dry, make a tiny black dot in the center using a black marking pen. Wrap the wires as desired, and glue the jack-o'-lantern and bat into place. Pin the arms into place. For the tall gourd, place the orange wire coil into position. Glue the right foam hand over the wire. Slip the hat brim over the top of the short gourd. Paint the gourd black above the brim. Slip the purple wire into place.

Take a Swing Piñata

MATERIALS

- 15-inch balloon
- 3 cups white flour
- Newspapers
- Colored papers: black, purple, yellow, and orange
- Party hat in metallic blue
- Paper punch
- Silver eyelets and eyelet tool
- Lime-green plastic lace
- 2 yards of ¼-inch-wide ribbon
- Crepe paper: orange and green

DIRECTIONS

Inflate and knot the balloon and set in a bowl. To make the papier-mache mixture, pour flour into a bowl. Stir in water until the mixture has the consistency of thick gravy. Tear the newspapers into strips. Dip one strip at a time in the flour mixture. Cover the balloon with two to three layers of paper strips, leaving only the balloon knot exposed. Turn balloon over in bowl and repeat; let dry. Remove balloon from bowl. Puncture the balloon and remove.

Enlarge and trace the patterns. Cut out the patterns. Trace around the patterns on colored papers and cut out.

Trace around the eye patterns in the eye area on the balloon. Use a crafts knife to cut out the eyes, cutting them slightly smaller than the traced eye area.

Glue the black pieces to the yellow eyes and the purple stripes to the hands and legs. Cut a 10-inch circle from black paper for the hat brim. Place the party hat in the center of the paper circle. Trace around the party hat. Cut out slightly inside the circle. Glue the party hat to the brim. Using the pattern as a guide, punch holes along the tops of both shoes.

Use an eyelet tool to secure eyelets in each hole as shown. Cut two 24-inch lengths of plastic lace. Lace through eyelets and tie ends into a bow. Glue the shoes to the legs.

Use a crafts knife to cut two small holes in the top of the piñata. Insert ribbon into needle. Sew through holes in piñata top. Knot the ribbon ends to secure. Wrap the crepe paper into a 1-foot loop. Carefully cut ½-inch-wide fringes along one side of the loop. Beginning at the large end of the piñata, wind and glue unfringed edge of the fringe onto the piñata. Continue until the piñata is covered. Pleat the arms. Fill the piñata with treats through the cutout eye areas. Glue the paper pieces onto the piñata, covering cutout eye areas with a paper eye. Tie a bow from green crepe paper. Glue onto the hat.

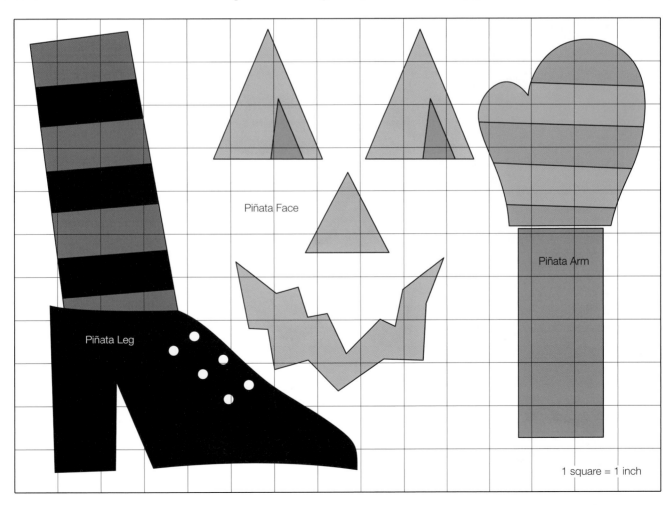

Piñata Face

Piñata Arm

Piñata Leg

1 square = 1 inch

Take a Seat

A homemade compilation CD filled with festive Halloween tunes turns into an eye-catching place card, above. Use a computer to create a message and print it onto Halloween-theme scrapbook papers. Cut the card out with pinking shears and add a ribbon to wrap the card around the CD. For fun, embellish the package with a plastic spider or other Halloween trinket.

Cheshire Cat

Black cats are a scary Halloween symbol, but one with a grin this wide, *above,* can't be all bad. Start with purchased brown kraft postcards and use our pattern, *page 104,* to trace the cat onto colored papers. A red sticker forms the nose; the background dots, swirls, cat's teeth lines, and whiskers are drawn with marking pens. Write the party information on the back of each card.

Halloween Dare

This invitation, *top,* may separate the 'fraidy cats from the daredevils among your invited guests. Start with folded paper, and top with an angled overlay of another color (black over purple on our invitation). Use a computer to print out the words in varying sizes and fonts. If you prefer, hand-letter the invitation or cut the message letters or words from old magazines. Write the party information on the inside of the card.

Waving Skeleton

While some skeleton figures look gruesome, this one, *above,* sports a large smile and a friendly wave. Trace the patterns of the card shape, *page 105,* the skeleton's head, and the bow tie; then cut them from colored papers. Place and glue the head on the card. Draw the arms, ribs, and facial features with markers. Decorate the bow as desired, and glue it on. Glue a paper strip to the card and write "All Dressed Up …" on the card front. Inside, write "And Somewhere to Go!" and the party information.

Arts & Crafts

So you don't know a Monet from a Manet? Not to worry. Neither do your guests. But they'll appreciate your masterpiece: a well-stocked arts-and-crafts table. Provide buckets of ribbons, pipe cleaners, markers, crayons, felt, glitter, and other crafty materials. Just make sure you have enough supplies for everyone.

For Halloween, masks or hats are perfect projects: easy-to-make and instantly put into play. **Tip:** For safety, cut out basic shapes ahead of time or have an adult at hand to help.

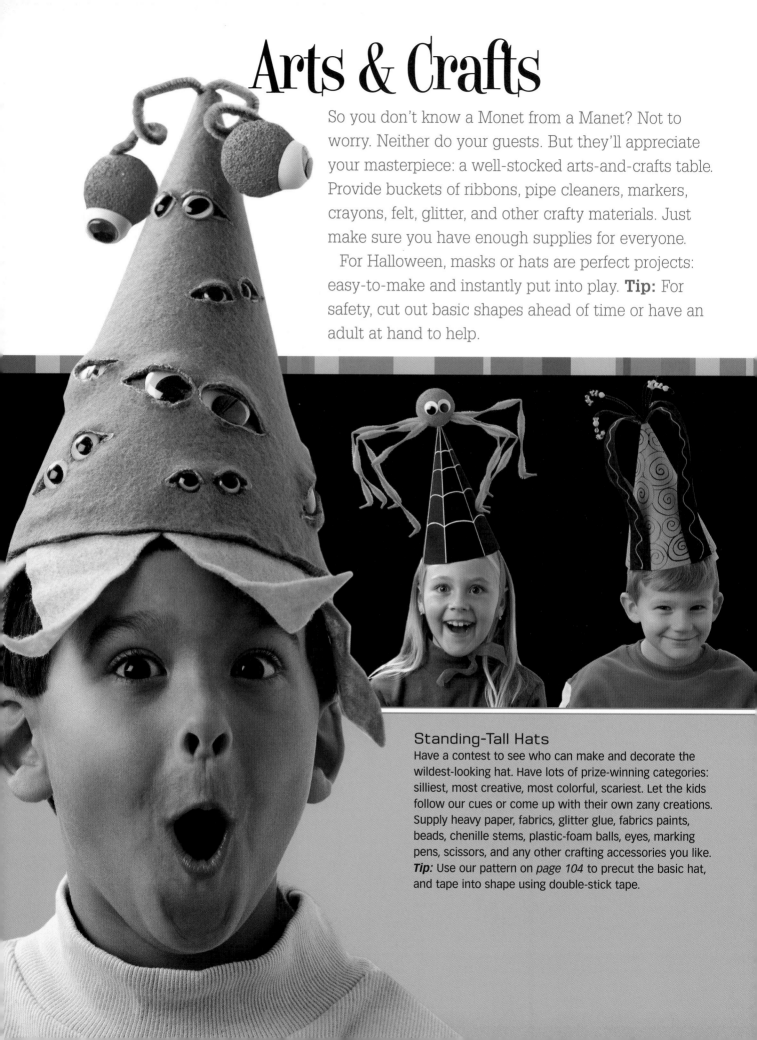

Standing-Tall Hats
Have a contest to see who can make and decorate the wildest-looking hat. Have lots of prize-winning categories: silliest, most creative, most colorful, scariest. Let the kids follow our cues or come up with their own zany creations. Supply heavy paper, fabrics, glitter glue, fabrics paints, beads, chenille stems, plastic-foam balls, eyes, marking pens, scissors, and any other crafting accessories you like. *Tip:* Use our pattern on *page 104* to precut the basic hat, and tape into shape using double-stick tape.

GYM CLASS

Kids are active—that's a given. Plan some or all of these activities geared to keep them on the move:

 Turn up the volume on the music and have a dance contest. Let the winner be first in line when it's time to eat.

 Write the names of Halloween characters on slips of paper: Frankenstein's monster, ghosts, vampires, zombies, witches, black cats, for example. Fold the papers and put into a basket. Let the kids take turns choosing a paper and act out the characters for others to guess.

 Let kids show off their muscles as they take turns swinging at a homemade pumpkin piñata. For the scoop on how to make this one, check out *page 102*.

 Make up a riddle or map to send kids on a treasure hunt. Hide clues for a hidden key, which unlocks a chest full of booty.

Mask-arade

Start with silver, black, or orange paper plates and end with … well, whatever silly creatures the kids choose. Have adult helpers assist in marking and cutting eyeholes and a nose notch. Use a marker to draw the holes—no cutting while the mask is on the child's face! Then cut the paper plates in any shape that suits. Use a crafts knife to cut out the eyeholes. Let the kids go wild adding feathers, sequins, chenille stems, pom-poms, glitter glue, and curling ribbon. Glue a 12-inch wooden dowel to the edge of each mask as a hand-hold.

> Kids love to see adults having fun, too, so ask grown-up hosts and helpers to don costumes for the party.

Say Cheese!

PHOTOGRAPHY LESSONS

Those costumes are too cute and clever to just be seen once. When the party's over, upload your digital photos to a site such as www.kodakgallery.com and make an online slide show so viewers can relive every funny moment.

Provide inexpensive cameras and let the kids snap the pics. They will ham it up for each other, guaranteeing funny, memorable photos.

Home "Eek"

Start with easy recipes. The fun of Halloween foods is in the details of decorating and naming. Punch isn't just plain ol' punch—it can be "Witch's Brew" or "Mummy Potion." And an everyday plain-Jane cupcake transforms into a spooky spider with just a little imagination and a few yummy ingredients.

Spider Cupcakes
Kids will love these tasty arachnids—bakery or box-mix cupcakes with tinted frosting topped with gumdrops and black string licorice. Attach the licorice legs to the gumdrops, and dab on frosting eyes. Finish with a sprinkle of edible glitter if you like.

Ghoulish Goblets
These glasses playfully dare guests to take a gulp. Start with clean, dry glassware; apply large sticker letters first and then top with the smaller letters. Add shiny sticker stars and fill 'em up. Loopy straws and ribbons tied around the stems make slurping lots of fun.

MUSIC CLASS
Good tunes are a must. Download your faves onto an MP3 player or iPod, and plug the player into your speakers. Pump your playlist full of these Halloween classics:

"THE TIME WARP"

"Werewolves of London"

"GHOSTBUSTERS"

"Monster Mash"

Serve up some healthy snack options along with the usual sweet and salty treats. Parents will thank you for including a few nutritious fruits, veggies, cheese cubes, and juices.

Pizza-pede

Tickle the kids' funnybones by having them help create this incredible edible insect. Each child can fill and decorate his or her own "body" segment. The crust is easily made from flattened refrigerated biscuits, while the "paints" are mixed up from egg yolks with drops of food coloring.

Pizza-pede

    3   egg yolks, discard egg whites
        Red, green, and yellow liquid food coloring
    3   teaspoons water
    2   7.5-ounce packages refrigerated biscuits
    1   18-ounce can pizza sauce
    1   13.5-ounce package sliced pepperoni
    1   18-ounce package shredded mozzarella cheese
    1   cup coarsely shredded carrot
    1   small tomato and parsley sprig
    2   pimiento-stuffed green olives

1. Place egg yolks in three small bowls. Add 1 teaspoon water and several drops of the desired food coloring to each bowl. Beat each egg mixture with a fork until well combined; set aside.

2. On a lightly floured surface, flatten each biscuit to a 4-inch circle, using hands or a rolling pin.

3. Place a small amount of pizza sauce (about 1 tablespoon) up to ¼ inch from the edge of one of the flattened biscuits. Top with pepperoni and cheese.

4. Place a few carrot shreds around the edge of the biscuit, forming legs.

5. Wet the edge of the biscuit with water. Top it with another flattened biscuit and press edges of biscuits together with fingers to seal.

6. Paint the top of the biscuit with colored egg mixtures. Place on lightly greased baking sheet. Repeat with remaining biscuits. Bake in a 375°F oven for 10 to 12 minutes.

7. Meanwhile, cut a small slice from the bottom of the tomato. Attach olives to the tomato with toothpicks to form eyes. Press in two shreds of carrot for antennae. Top the head with a parsley sprig, and arrange to form the pizza-pede.

Dancing Skeletons

Get guests in the party mood with these happy-go-lucky skeletons who never seem to miss a beat. You'll have plenty of time to dance yourself since the tumblers are quick and easy to embellish using paint markers—no bones about it! Instructions, page 103.

Serve up individual portions of foods in kid-friendly ways—including placing cookies and bars on napkins—to make them easy to grab-and-go.

Dish up dips in tiny paper or plastic cups to avoid double-dipping, and skewer cheese cubes and fruit with toothpicks topped with tiny plastic bugs or spiders.

Mark disposable beverage glasses with the kids' names so they can reuse them.

Icky Ice Ring

Any punch-bowl beverage can become home to a swarm of gross bugs and other Halloween critters—the sight may freeze your party guests in their tracks. To make an ice ring, wash plastic bugs, snakes, or other creatures in hot soapy water. Rinse well. Arrange as you like in the bottom of a 6-cup ring mold. Slowly add unsweetened juice (the same kind you'll use in the punch) or water to cover the plastic pieces. Freeze until firm; then fill the mold with juice or water and freeze again.

Recess

A treasure hunt can take on nearly any party theme, such as pirates seeking gold doubloons (chocolate coins wrapped in foil) or a Hansel-and-Gretel hunt for the witch's gingerbread cookies.

Treasure Hunt
Concoct a riddle to set off the hunt, divide the children into teams to start their search, and set them off in all directions in search of additional clues … and the loot.

Don't forget the old-fashioned games. In these days of high-tech toys, such activities as bobbing for apples, three-legged races, and egg-and-spoon relays offer novelty and appeal.

FINAL EXAM

It's time to put your party skills to the test one last time—and how will you know if you passed? Consider yourself at the top of the class if you hear guests ask, "When's the next party?"

For extra credit (and easy clean-up), include a cleanup game or contest, engaging the kids as eager helpers. If you have plenty of trash cans with liners decorated as ghosts or pumpkins, they'll have a fun time stashing their trash.

One more way to ensure honors status—send the kids home with favors prepared in advance. Include such treats as jelly beans, chocolates, trail mix, caramel corn, or gum balls and such trinkets as keychains, stickers, or novelty pencils.

Pumpkin Piñata
For a smashing good time at your Halloween get-together, make and fill a pumpkin piñata. Start with a round balloon, then layer on strips of papier-mâché, and finally glue on a great big grin to hint at all the goodies that hide within. Instructions, page 102.

lights out!

DIM THE LIGHTS
Add magic to nighttime parties with flashlights, flickering lightbulbs, or strands of special Halloween lights.

If kids of various ages will be at the party, skew the rules of the games a bit so they all get to play and the little ones have as much chance of winning as the older kids. For example, for every age level, add another step to a relay race.

Take-Home Treats

As the party winds down, pull out a batch of goodie bags and let the kids each pick one to take home as they head out the door.

Cone-Cup Containers
Start with cone-shape drinking cups; spray-paint them black or another color. Use silver and gold pens to write Halloween sayings and draw swirls and dots or apply brightly colored stickers. Add ribbon or hot-glued handles; fill with candies or popcorn.

FREE GHOST TO A GOOD HOME!

Ghost Bags
Kids can see right through these ghostly bags to the treats contained within. Use vellum bags and simply glue on google eyes. After filling the bags, lace them shut with long ribbons of black plastic string.

Cat and Spider Treat Cups
Give plain plastic cups iridescence with the addition of glass paints and flat marbles. Instructions, page 103.

Pumpkin Piñata

MATERIALS

- 20-inch-diameter oval or round balloon
- Ruler
- Newspaper
- Sponge brush
- Mod Podge decoupage medium
- Sharp knife
- Candy and small plastic and paper toys
- Tissue papers: Orange, light green, and dark green
- Black-and-white polka-dot scrapbook paper
- Paintbrushes
- Acrylic paints: brown and orange
- Green raffia
- Wooden dowels: 12 inches of ¼-inch diameter and 36 inches of ⅝-inch diameter
- Microwave oven
- Hot-glue gun and hotmelt adhesive
- Green twist paper
- Black webbing spray paint

INSTRUCTIONS

1. Blow up the balloon and tie it off in a knot. Tear newspaper into 2×4-inch strips to cover the balloon.

2. Using a sponge brush, cover a small area of the balloon with decoupage medium. Lay newspaper strips over the area, overlapping the strips as you work. Brush more medium over the newspaper strips. Continue in this manner until the balloon is completely covered.

3. Cut five or more 1×4-inch strips of newspaper for a hanging loop. Glue the strips together and to the balloon with the decoupage medium. Let the paper dry completely.

4. Tear 2×4-inch strips of orange tissue paper. Except for the hanging loop, decoupage the entire piñata with tissue-paper strips as directed in step 2. Let the paper dry completely.

5. Cut out the face pattern, *below,* from scrapbook paper. Using decoupage medium, glue the features to the front of the piñata. Paint the hanging loop brown, and let it dry.

6. Pull out several strands of green raffia, and dampen them with water. Wrap the raffia around the small wooden dowel, and place it in a microwave oven for about 30 seconds or until the raffia is dry (do not leave the oven unattended). Hot-glue the raffia vines to the top of the piñata.

7. Cut eleven 4-inch lengths of green twist paper. Unwrap one length and set it aside. Then unwrap all but 1 inch of one end of the other lengths for the pumpkin leaves. Cut three V shapes along the untwisted ends. Glue the twisted

ends to the piñata around the hanging loop. In the center of the unwrapped length, cut a small square. Then cut three or four V shapes along each side. Glue the shape over the hanging loop, covering the untwisted ends of the leaves.

8. Use a sharp knife to cut a three-sided flap in the back of the piñata. Fill the shape with candy and small toys. Seal the opening with tissue-paper strips.

Pumpkin Piñata Face Pattern

Cat and Spider Treat Cups

MATERIALS

Clear plastic punch cups
Tracing paper
Tape
Glass paints: Black, green, yellow, and white
Paintbrush
Flat glass marbles: Iridescent black and frosted clear or pale green
Silicone glue

INSTRUCTIONS

1. Wash and dry the cups. Avoid touching the areas to be painted.

2. If painting the cat, trace the pattern, *right,* onto tracing paper. Cut out slightly beyond the drawn lines. Tape the pattern to the inside of the cup where you wish to paint the design. Place it low on the cup so the weight of the eyes does not tip the cup.

3. To make the cat cup, paint the cat black. Let the paint dry. Referring to the photograph, paint on the nose, mouth, and whisker details. To paint the marble eyes, mix a drop of green and yellow. Paint long ovals on the front sides of two frosted marbles. Let the paint dry. Paint smaller black ovals inside of the green ones. Let the paint dry. Glue the eyes in place and let dry.

4. To make the spider, glue two iridescent black marbles on the cup. Place them low enough so the cup does not tip. Let the glue dry. Paint on black legs; let dry.

Cat Treat Cup Pattern

Dancing Skeleton Glass

MATERIALS

Tracing paper
Glass or plastic tumbler with somewhat flat side
Waterproof paint markers: black and white

INSTRUCTIONS

1. Trace the desired dancing skeleton onto tracing paper. Cut out the shape 1/2 inch from the design.

2. Tape the traced shape inside the tumbler so the image faces out.

3. Use the pattern lines as guides to draw the skeleton bones and facial features with the black paint marker; let dry.

4. Add details with the white marker; let dry. *(Note: We recommend hand-washing the tumbler.)*

Skeleton Patterns

Cheshire Cat Invitation Pattern

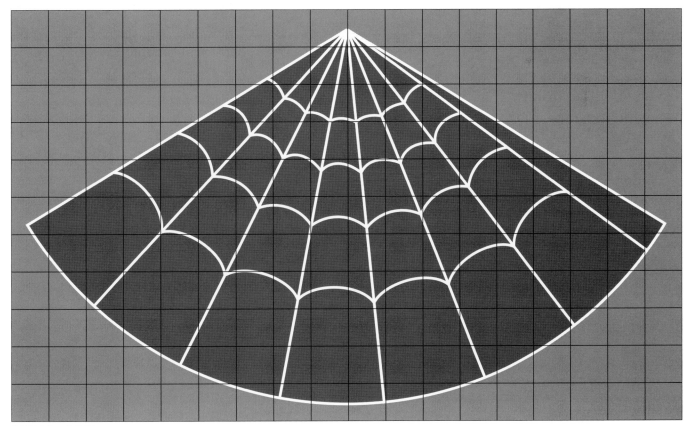

1 Square = 1 Inch

Standing Tall Hat Pattern

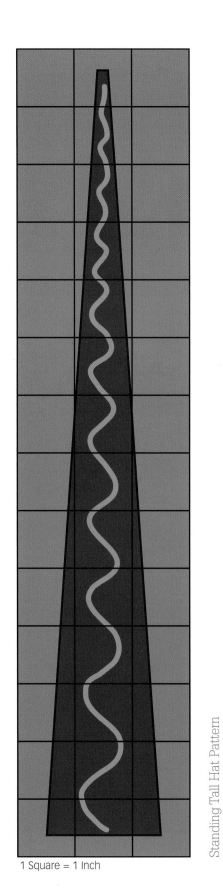

1 Square = 1 Inch

Standing Tall Hat Pattern

All Dressed Up...

Waving Skeleton Invitation Pattern

costumes

Get your little ghosts and goblins into the Halloween spirit with this collection of imaginative costumes that are surprisingly easy to create.

a cast of cute

Mice, bugs, bees, and frogs may not be the most cuddly critters around, but dress your kids up in these cute costumes and they'll hear only "ooh" and "aah" as they scamper from door to door trick-or-treating.

lovely ladybug

Start with basic black pants, a shirt, and gloves; add lightweight polka-dot wings and an antennae-topped stocking cap. Your child will be cute as a bug as she flits from door to door.

creatures

MATERIALS

Pencil
Tracing paper
Scissors
¼-inch-thick red crafts foam
Thin black crafts foam
Glue gun and hotmelt adhesive
Paper punch
4 eyelets and eyelet punch
Pair of black 42-inch-long shoelaces
Black chenille stem
Two large black pom-poms

INSTRUCTIONS

Enlarge and trace the wing pattern, *page 115*, onto tracing paper. Cut out. Trace the dot pattern, *page 115*, and cut out. Cut two wings from the red foam and six dots from the black foam. Glue the short flat edges of the wings together. Glue three dots on each wing. Let the glue dry. Use a paper punch to make two holes at the top of each wing. For reinforcement, add an eyelet to each. Tie the shoelaces together at one end. Place the knot by the seam on the wrong side of the wings. Thread the laces through the holes in each wing.

For the antennae, poke a chenille stem through a pair of holes at the top of the hat and glue a pom-pom on each end. Let dry.

busy bee

Make this bold-stripe costume in various sizes; just enlarge the pattern accordingly. Fashion a whole swarm of them so the entire family can fly from the hive together.

MATERIALS

Tracing paper
Pencil
Scissors
24×48-inch piece of heavy sew-in interfacing
3 yards of 72-inch-wide black felt
¼ yard of 72-inch-wide yellow felt
Spray adhesive
Thick white crafts glue
6 yards of yellow medium rickrack
3 black extrathick chenille stems
Black headband
Two 2-inch yellow pom-poms
Yellow gloves, black leggings or sweatpants, black turtleneck sweater or sweatshirt

INSTRUCTIONS

Enlarge and trace the patterns, *page 116*. Cut two tabards from the interfacing and four from the black felt. Cut two stingers from the yellow felt. Layer the interfacing tabards between the felt tabards, using spray adhesive to temporarily secure the layers. Machine-zigzag around the neck and outer edges. Cut six 3×22-inch yellow felt strips. Glue the strips to the tabard as indicated on the pattern. Trim the ends to match the tabard. Glue yellow rickrack around the neck and outer edges. Stitch an 18-inch-long piece of yellow rickrack to each side at the X's to make ties.

Glue the stinger points together, sandwiching one end of a chenille stem between them. Stitch the other end of the chenille stem to the dot on the tabard back. For antennae, twist one end of each remaining chenille stem around the tip of the headband. Glue a pom-pom to each tip. Let dry.

Dress the child in the black pants, black shirt, and yellow gloves. Slip the tabard over the child's head. Place the antennae headband on the child's head.

Each COSTUME requires only SIMPLE sewing SKILLS and a few BASIC supplies.

MATERIALS

Scissors
Ruler
¼ yard of green felt
Fabrics glue
Green hooded sweat suit, gloves, and swim fins
2 table-tennis balls
Permanent black marking pen

INSTRUCTIONS

Cut nine 6-inch-long triangles from the green felt. With the narrow points down, glue the triangles around the sweatshirt at the neck area right below the hood. Let dry.

Cut two 4×7-inch pieces from the felt. Align the center of one long edge with the center of a table-tennis ball. Shape and glue the felt to the ball at the top and sides. Let dry.

Draw a dime-size dot in the middle of each table-tennis ball. Draw a slanted 1-inch-long line through each dot. Glue the eyes to top of the hood. Let dry.

Dress the child in the sweat suit, gloves, and swim fins.

ready-to-leap frog

Hop into holiday fun with this frog costume. It's especially easy to be green this Halloween.

For family FUN, dress in a grown-up version of your child's pint-size COSTUME.

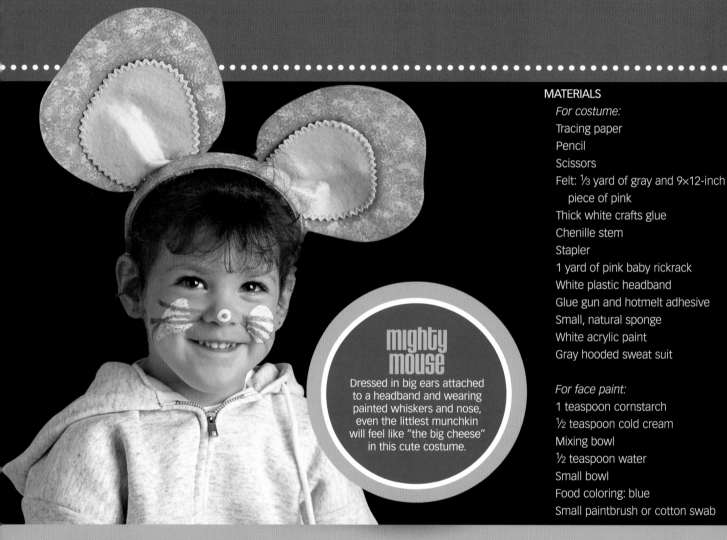

mighty mouse

Dressed in big ears attached to a headband and wearing painted whiskers and nose, even the littlest munchkin will feel like "the big cheese" in this cute costume.

MATERIALS

For costume:
Tracing paper
Pencil
Scissors
Felt: 1/3 yard of gray and 9×12-inch piece of pink
Thick white crafts glue
Chenille stem
Stapler
1 yard of pink baby rickrack
White plastic headband
Glue gun and hotmelt adhesive
Small, natural sponge
White acrylic paint
Gray hooded sweat suit

For face paint:
1 teaspoon cornstarch
1/2 teaspoon cold cream
Mixing bowl
1/2 teaspoon water
Small bowl
Food coloring: blue
Small paintbrush or cotton swab

INSTRUCTIONS

Enlarge and trace the mouse inner ear and outer ear patterns, *page 116,* and cut out. Cut two outer ears from the gray felt. Cut two inner ears from the pink felt. Glue an inner ear atop each outer ear, sandwiching and gluing half of a chenille stem from top to bottom between each set of ears so you can bend them. Tuck each ear under the headband, securing with a staple along the bottom edge. Glue rickrack around the outer edge of each inner ear.

Cut a strip of gray felt the length and width of the headband. Glue the strip around the top of the headband, trimming as necessary to match the edges. Bend the bottom 1 inch of each ear forward at a 90-degree angle. Hot-glue the bent portion of each ear to the underside of the headband. Dip a moist sponge into a puddle of the white acrylic paint; sponge-paint on the ears and headband. Let the paint dry.

For face paint, stir together the cornstarch and cold cream in a mixing bowl until it is well blended. Add water and stir. Put about half of the cold-cream mixture into a small bowl. Add food coloring, one drop at a time, to one of the portions until the desired color is achieved. Mix well. Using the photograph, *above,* for inspiration, paint the cheeks and nose with the white cold-cream mixture using a paintbrush or cotton swab. Add whiskers and other details with the blue cold-cream mixture.

Dress the child in the gray sweat suit. Paint the child's face; slip the headband on the child's head.

MATERIALS

- 60×60-inch piece of black fabric
- White sewing pencil
- Scissors
- Straightedge
- Fusible facing
- Elastic
- Sequin trim: silver and red
- Thread
- Black buttons
- Purchased black sweatshirt, black leggings or sweatpants, bat ears, white gloves, white socks, and plastic fangs

bootiful bat

Wrap fanciful wings around your trick-or-treater as part of this simply batty getup. Accent the child's cheeks with a dab of face paint and his or her lips with red lipstick.

INSTRUCTIONS

Fold the fabric in half to form a triangle. Using the photograph, *above*, for inspiration, draw curves around the edges of the fabric with the sewing pencil. Cut out the wings through both layers using the diagram, *page 116*. While the fabric is still folded, cut out a center half circle for the neck. Adjust the size of the cape at the arms and head opening to fit the child. Using a straightedge, draw lines from the curved points to the fold on both the front and back of the costume to form the wing struts.

Fuse the facing inside the neck opening. Make small slits about 1½ inches apart in the neck facing.

Thread the elastic through the slits; adjust to fit loosely around the child's neck. Sew the ends together.

Stitch a single row of silver sequin trim along each strut line on the wing front and back. Stitch red sequin trim around the bottom edge. Fit the wings cape on the child. Sew two sets of black buttons at the underarms through both layers as shown to secure the cape.

Dress the child in the sweat suit, socks, gloves, wings, ears, and fangs.

cute creatures

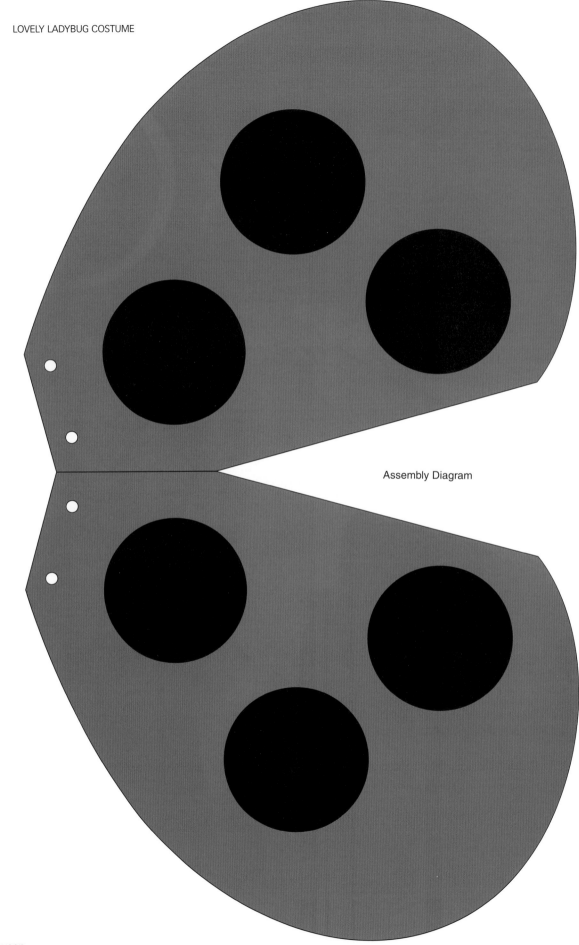

Assembly Diagram

WING AND DOT PATTERNS

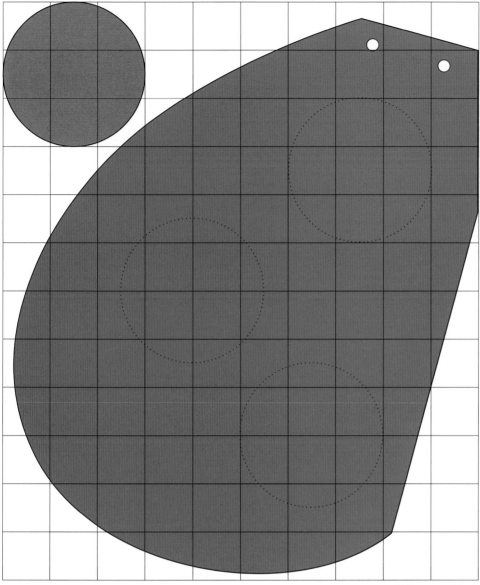

1 Square = 1 Inch

cute creatures

BUSY BEE COSTUME

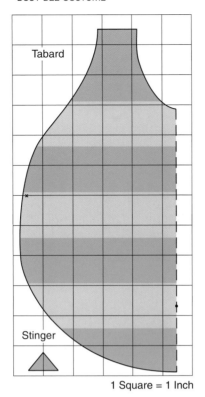

Tabard

Stinger

1 Square = 1 Inch

MIGHTY MOUSE COSTUME

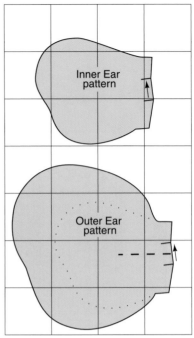

Inner Ear pattern

Outer Ear pattern

1 Square = 1 Inch

BAT COSTUME

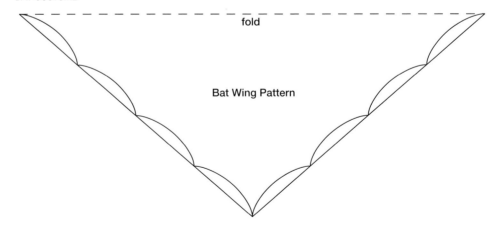

fold

Bat Wing Pattern

Pair basic kids' apparel with a few pieces of sparkly fabric, fuzzy faux fur, and cleverly embellished accessories to conjure up some spirited trick-or-treating attire.

Costume
Tricks That Treat

DESIGNED BY HEIDI BOYD   WRITTEN BY KRISTIN SCHMITT
PHOTOGRAPHED BY BLAINE MOATS

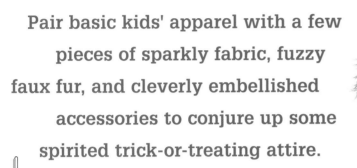

Starstruck

Rock your little diva's world with this sizzling ensemble that's born from modest beginnings—khaki pants and a pink T-shirt. From the hot-pink print vest to the sparkling star patches, a little fabrics glue is all you'll need to get the right look. Then let your ambitious star help you accessorize her attire for the big encore.

Living in Fairyland

Delight your Tinkerbell fan with her own fairy rendition that makes her the queen of the butterfly forest. As easily as she can sprinkle pixie dust with a wave of her magic wand, you can embellish a green cotton skirt and bolero with layers of tulle and pretty silk flowers. Crown your friendly fairy with a headband adorned with flowers and butterflies.

If costume shops bore you and elaborate patterns scare you, let these clever costume creations put the treat back into Halloween.

Sweet as a Rose

You've never seen such a sweet-smelling skunk as your little mademoiselle in this cuddly costume. Making her attire is as easy as gluing black and white feather boas to a black fleece sweat suit, with pretty pink touches for added appeal.

Spread Your Wings and Fly

Don't go batty trying to sew from scratch a head-to-toe ensemble for your little one's outing. Turn her into a winged critter cute enough to squeeze by tacking pieces of sequined fabric to a basic black top. Those sonar-sensitive ears are simply fabric attached to a newsboy-style cap.

All-Play Zone

No need for heavy construction here. Zip ties and hot glue easily attach the playful roads and trucks to an orange T-shirt uniform. Add a road sign, top with a petite soccer cone mounted on a baseball cap, and you're on the road to an all-play-and-no-work Halloween celebration.

Rock Star Diva

MATERIALS

- ½ yard pink cheetah fabric
- Feather boas: black and bright pink
- Glue gun and hotmelt adhesive
- Tan pants
- Scraps of pink and purple sequined fabric
- Black felt
- Fabrics glue
- Sunglasses and assorted rhinestone stars
- Crafts glue
- 2½-inch plastic-foam ball and serrated knife
- Silver glitter
- 7-inch length each of ¾-inch-diameter wooden dowel and ¾-inch-diameter pipe insulation
- Black duct tape
- Black crafts foam

INSTRUCTIONS

Enlarge and trace the vest front and back patterns; cut out two fronts (one reversed) and one back from cheetah fabric. With right sides facing and using a ½-inch seam allowance, sew the vest fronts to the back at the shoulders and sides. Turn under a 1-inch seam allowance on the fronts and the lower bottom edge; hem in place. Hot-glue short lengths of black boa around the neck and arm openings.

Hot-glue pieces of bright pink boa around the bottom of each pant leg. Cut out three large stars and one small star from sequin fabrics. Use fabrics glue to adhere the sequin stars to black felt; cut out ¼ inch around the sequin stars. Glue the stars to the pants, referring to the photograph for placement.

Glue rhinestones to the sunglasses. To make the microphone top, trim ¼ inch from one side of the plastic-foam ball with a serrated knife. Brush crafts glue over the round portion and sprinkle silver glitter over the wet glue; let dry.

For the microphone handle, cover the wooden dowel with pipe insulation. Cover the insulation with duct tape. Cut three 3½-inch-diameter circles from black crafts foam. Cut a circle opening at the center of each foam circle large enough to accommodate the finished microphone handle. Thread the crafts-foam circles over one end of the handle and hot-glue the silver ball to the top.

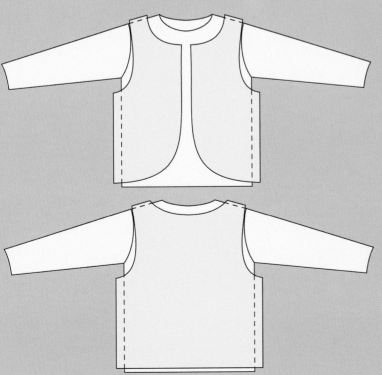

Bat

MATERIALS

Black sweatshirt and pants
1½ yards of gold-and-black dot metallic fabric
Black fun fur
Glue gun and hotmelt adhesive
Flat cotton hat
Polyester fiberfill

INSTRUCTIONS

Lay out the sweatshirt on a flat surface and measure from the center to the end of one cuff. Enlarge and trace the wing pattern so it is as wide as this measurement. Fold over one cut end of the metallic fabric to create a double layer of fabric to accommodate the pattern. Cut out the wings through both layers; do not cut on the fold. Unfold the wings and tack the top corners to the cuffs of the sweatshirt.

Enlarge and trace the yoke pattern to the size needed to cover the front of the sweatshirt. Make a second yoke pattern, trimming off about half of the length on the front of the pattern. Fold the remaining metallic fabric in half; cut out each yoke. Position the large yoke right side down on the sweatshirt front; then place the small yoke wrong side down on the first. Tack the yokes to the sweatshirt at the shoulders, the front and back neck edges, and the center bottom on the front. Tack the center top of the wings to the center bottom of the larger yoke. Hot-glue black fun fur around the top of the layered yokes to cover the neck edges.

Cover the cap with a large piece of metallic fabric; fold the fabric to the inside of the cap and hot-glue in place.

Cut out two triangular-shape ears from a double layer of metallic fabric. Sew the ears together in pairs, leaving the bottom edge open. Turn the ears right

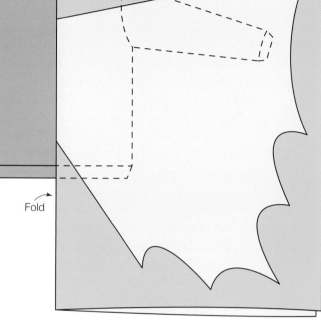
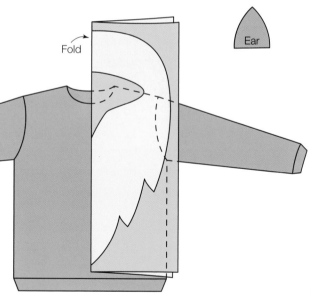

side out and stuff with fiberfill. Hand-sew the ears to the cap. Hot-glue a triangle of black fun fur to the front of each ear.

Woodland Fairy

MATERIALS

Heavyweight florist's wire and wire cutters
Fabric-covered headband
Two 2×4¾-inch sheer butterflies on clips
1 silk spring flower garland
Glue gun and hotmelt adhesive
Green cotton jersey bolero and elastic-waist skirt
Fabrics glue
Nylon tulle: 2 yards each of dark, medium, and light
    pink and green

INSTRUCTIONS

Cut a 20-inch length of florist's wire; fold in half. Tightly twist the wires together 3 to 4 inches from the center fold. Position the twisted wire over the top of the headband; wrap the untwisted wire around the headband to secure. Repeat with a second 20-inch length of wire, twisting the wires together 2 to 3 inches from the center fold. Clip a butterfly to the end of each twisted wire. Hot-glue a short length of silk flower garland to the top of the headband, covering the wire wraps.

Lay the bolero flat; place paper inside to prevent glue from bleeding through. Glue flower garland along the neck and center front edges of the bolero; let dry.

Work with one color of tulle at a time to make the skirt. Fold one piece in half lengthwise with the fold at the top. This folded edge will be at the waist of the skirt. Fold the length of tulle widthwise in half, quarters, and then eighths. Using the diagram as a guide, cut pointed petal tips. Adjust the length of the piece so it will extend 3 to 5 inches below the skirt. Unfold the tulle and sew a long gathering stitch close to the waistband fold. Pull the threads to gather the tulle until it fits around the waistband of the skirt. Repeat for each piece of tulle.

Stack the gathered tulle skirt pieces. Position the layered tulle skirt pieces on the skirt; pin in place. Sew the tulle pieces to the skirt, sewing atop the gathering line. Use fabrics glue to attach the flower garland around the skirt.

Folded Top

Folded Sides

Construction-Zone Boy

MATERIALS

Oversize orange T-shirt

Gray sweatshirt

Four 1×30-inch strips of 120-grit aluminum
 oxide sanding belt

6 assorted lightweight plastic trucks

Plastic cable ties: orange and yellow

Glue gun and hotmelt adhesive

Two 9-inch squares of bright yellow foam core

Black permanent marker

Black duct tape

8-inch square of green indoor/outdoor carpeting

Orange baseball hat

Child-size plastic soccer cone

Additional costume accessories: foam
 knee pads and child's leather work gloves

INSTRUCTIONS

Place the gray sweatshirt inside the orange T-shirt, lining up the seams and laying the garments flat. Position a sanding-belt strip over one shoulder of the T-shirt for a road, angling the ends toward the center front and back of the shirt. To attach a vehicle, use a scissors to make a small hole through both garment layers on each side of the road. Thread a yellow cable tie through the holes and use it to secure the vehicle and road to the garments. Repeat to attach a belt over the remaining shoulder and one belt at each side of the T-shirt bottom, referring to the photo, *page 120,* for vehicle placement. Trim the belts if necessary and use hot glue to secure the ends to the T-shirt.

Round the corners of the yellow foam-core squares. Use the black permanent marker to draw a road-sign image on each foam-core square, referring to the photo. Apply a strip of duct tape vertically on the back of each sign for reinforcement. Poke two holes an inch apart at the top and bottom of each sign. Plan the placement of the signs on the garment front and back and make holes through the garments to align with the holes in the signs. Secure the signs to the garment with orange cable ties.

Place the carpet square on top of the baseball hat and position the cone on the carpet square. Use the scissors to make a set of holes 1 inch apart under a corner of the cone, cutting through both the carpet and the hat. Thread a yellow cable tie through the holes and use it to secure the cone and carpet on the hat. Repeat for each corner of the cone. Use the same technique to attach a vehicle to the hat brim.

Skunk

MATERIALS

½ yard of black fabric

White pencil

Polyester fiberfill

Black hooded full-zip sweatshirt and pants

Feather boas: 2 white and 2 black

Glue gun and hotmelt adhesive

¾ yard of striped ribbon

Scraps of light pink fun fur

2 pink silk flowers

INSTRUCTIONS

For the tail, fold the black fabric in half widthwise with right sides together. Draw an 18-inch-long petal shape and cut out. With right sides facing and using a ¼-inch seam allowance, sew the pieces together, leaving the top edge open. Turn the tail right side out and stuff with fiberfill. Hand-sew the tail just above the ribbing to the back of the sweatshirt.

Draw two triangular-shape ears on a double-layer of black fabric; cut out. Sew the ears together in pairs, leaving the bottom edge open. Turn right side out; stuff with fiberfill. Hand-sew the ears to the top of the hood.

For the stripe, fold one white boa in half and hot-glue it to the hood and the back of the sweatshirt. Hot-glue a black boa around the attached white boa.

Cut the ribbon in half and hot-glue one end of each ribbon just below the hood on the sweatshirt fronts. Cut the second white boa in half, and then fold each piece in half. Hot-glue one folded half to each side on the front of the sweatshirt, covering the attached ribbon ends and keeping the feathers free of the zipper.

Add trim to the bottom of the pants legs, the ears, and the underside of the tail with the second black boa. Hot-glue pink fun fur to the ears. Attach a pink silk flower to each pants leg.

A few basic pieces of kids' apparel and some crafts supplies are all it takes to whip up one of these winners.

Creative
CHARACTERS
FOR KIDS

you are my sunshine

A simple yellow sweat suit can be the springboard for other cheerful costume ideas. Add white feathers and a rubber beak to transform it into a chicken. Or tack orange chenille stems along the sides and a felt smiley face on the front to fashion a glowing sun.

Delightful Duck

There won't be any ruffled feathers over complicated sewing tasks when you fashion this happy-go-ducky outfit. A few quick hand stitches of a feather boa onto a hooded sweatshirt are all it takes. Complete the ensemble with yellow sweatpants and gloves—and don't forget the rubber galoshes for a splashing good time!

Rockin' Robot

Let your little science guy (or gal) engineer the components of an electronic persona. You build the base: foil-covered cardboard fastened with colored plastic coils for the body and a plastic paint can topped with a funnel for the cap. Then let your robotic kid construct a control panel by gluing on a variety of textured and dimensional accessories.

creativity in a box

Send this space-age costume back to Kansas by forgoing the control-panel accessories and you've got Dorothy's friend the Tin Man. Or paint the cardboard base and hat blue, red, or yellow, and glue plastic bowls to the front and back to construct a Lego block.

the more the merrier

The fun of Halloween dress-up is pretending to be something you're not. Use this spider idea to create other creatures. Try green fabric and short socks for a friendly caterpillar; or go purple, with as many arms as you imagine, to become a silly purple people-eater!

SPOOKY SPIDER

Think of the places a spider must be able to go with eight legs instead of two. What kid wouldn't delight in the prospect! This simply-sewn black shell worn over a dark turtleneck and leggings forms this costume's body, while stuffed socks and gloves grow into the additional appendages.

Delightful Duck

HERE'S WHAT YOU'LL NEED

Scissors
Yellow feather boa
Children's yellow sweat suit
Yellow sewing thread
Sewing needle
Yellow gloves
Yellow boots

HAVE FUN CRAFTING

Cut two pieces from the yellow feather boa, each long enough to stretch from the child's shoulder to the wrist. With yellow sewing thread, hand-stitch each piece in place on the topside of the sweatshirt sleeves.

Cut another piece of the feather boa approximately 5" long and hand-stitch it to the point of the hood. Add yellow gloves and yellow rubber boots to complete the costume.

DESIGNED BY BARBARA HALL PALAR

Rockin' Robot

HERE'S WHAT YOU'LL NEED

Medium-size cardboard box
Scissors
Aluminum foil
Plastic paint bucket
Blue plastic funnel
Glue gun and hotmelt adhesive
12" square of silver metallic fabric
Four to six 6" plastic coils
    in assorted colors
Miscellaneous items to create pattern
    and texture on the box (such as
    old telephone parts, buttons, self-
    adhesive reflectors, wire, circuit
    boards, clock parts, tubing from a
    hardware store, reflective adhesive
    tape, egg-carton cups covered with
    aluminum foil, metallic sequin trim,
    or disposable foil baking pans)
Wire cutters
Dryer-vent hose
Hook-and-loop fasteners

HAVE FUN CRAFTING

Cut out two sides of a cardboard box for the front and back. Cover the cardboard with aluminum foil.

For the helmet, cut out part of one side of the paint bucket so your child's face will show through. Using hotmelt adhesive, cover the bucket with aluminum foil and attach the funnel to the top.

Cut two 3×8" strips of silver metallic fabric. Use hotmelt adhesive to attach the strips to the top side edge of each piece of cardboard to create the shoulder straps.

Poke two holes in the midsection of each long side of the box. Insert each end of a length of coiled plastic into a hole in the front and back sides. Secure the coil with hotmelt adhesive. Attach three more lengths of coiled plastic in the same manner.

Embellish the hat and body pieces by gluing on some of the miscellaneous items noted in the supplies list. You can find many inexpensive, colorful items for decorating your costume at a local discount store.

Use wire cutters to cut two 8" lengths of dryer-vent hose for the armbands. Apply hook-and-loop fasteners to the edges of each armband and underneath the shoulder straps. After the child puts on the body piece, slip the armbands onto his arms. The fasteners will keep the arm bands in place.

DESIGNED BY GINGER HANSEN SHAFER

Spooky Spider

HERE'S WHAT YOU'LL NEED

Tracing paper
Scissors
2 yards of black broadcloth
2 yards of quilt batting
2 yards of black strapping
Black sewing thread
Sewing needle
Polyester fiberfill
3 pairs of children's black gloves
2 pairs of children's black
    knee-high socks
4 yards of ¼"-wide black ribbon
Black turtleneck
Black gloves
Black leggings or tights

HAVE FUN CRAFTING

Referring to the photo, *opposite,* for the shape, draw the spider body outline on a piece of paper and cut out. Using your pattern, cut four pieces from the black broadcloth and two pieces from the quilt batting, all on the fold.

Make the spider body: Place two of the black pieces with right sides together and one piece of quilt batting on the outside of one of the black pieces. Machine-stitch around the edges through all of the layers, leaving an opening for turning. Turn the piece right side out; slip-stitch the opening closed. Repeat with the remaining black pieces and quilt batting.

Pin two lengths of black strapping to the top of one of the body pieces, pinning the opposite ends to the second body piece. The straps should connect the front and back body pieces. Have your child try on the costume so you can lengthen or shorten the straps and position them as necessary. Attach the straps by hand-stitching them with black sewing thread.

Using fiberfill, stuff the fingers of four of the gloves and each sock. Slide the foot of each sock into a glove, and hand-sew the sock and glove together. Make four openings in the side seams of the front body panel large enough for the ends of the socks. The first set of openings should be 12" from the top; the second set should be 8" to 9" below the first. Stuff the socks into the openings, and hand-sew the socks to the front body panel. Using the black ribbon, hand-sew ties to each side of the costume. Have your child wear a black turtleneck, black gloves, and black leggings or tights to complete the costume.

DESIGNED BY BARBARA HALL PALAR

treats

Greet your party guests with freaky fare in keeping with the Halloween spirit. But don't let these treats in disguise fool you—they're not only fun to eat, they're tasty, too.

freaky food

This Halloween, whether you're planning an evening of enchanting entertaining or you simply want to add a little fun to ordinary fare, these spine-tingling snacks are sure to produce a howling good time.

FOOD STYLED BY DIANNA NOLIN   WRITTEN BY STACI SCHEURENBRAND   PHOTOGRAPHED BY MARTY BALDWIN

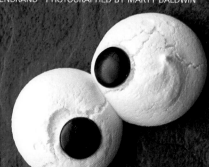

Spooky Smoothies

Add candy pupils to meringue drops and you'll have oogly, googly eyeballs to top off frightfully fruity smoothies.

Scaredy-Cat Ice Cream Cake
Guests of all ages will be clawing their way to the table to get their paws on this HISS-terically simple yet PURR-fectly delicious dessert made with brownie mix and ice cream.

Scary Skulls
Candy-coated and creepy, these skull-shape pears are a shuddersome substitute for traditional caramel apples.

Witch's Hat Calzones

Abracadabra gobbledygook ... gather pizza-type ingredients and you won't need to use hocus-pocus to make these bewitching treats disappear.

Tippy Tombstones
How do you make spirits rise?
Simply dig around the cereal
cupboard and whip up a batch of
cute and kooky graveyard grub.

Moody Monsters

Watch imaginations run wild as your little ghouls and goblins create their own monstrous muffin masterpieces.

Spooky Smoothies

- 1 6-ounce carton low-fat lemon yogurt
- 1 cup milk
- 1 cup frozen unsweetened blueberries
- 1 cup frozen unsweetened blackberries
- 1 to 2 tablespoons honey or sugar
   Ghostly Meringue Eyes

In a blender, combine yogurt, milk, blueberries, and blackberries. Cover and blend until smooth. Blend in desired amount of honey. Pour into glasses. Serve immediately with Ghostly Meringue Eyes. Makes 2 or 3 servings.

Ghostly Meringue Eyes: Place 2 egg whites in a large mixing bowl; let them stand at room temperature for 30 minutes. Preheat oven to 300°F. Line two large baking sheets with foil or parchment paper; set aside.

Add ½ teaspoon vanilla and ⅛ teaspoon cream of tartar to egg whites. Beat with an electric mixer on medium speed until soft peaks form. Gradually add ⅔ cup sugar, 1 tablespoon at a time, beating about 4 minutes on high speed until stiff peaks form and sugar is almost dissolved.

Place meringue in a pastry bag fitted with a ½-inch round tip. Pipe meringue onto the prepared baking sheets in pairs of 1- to 2-inch mounds that touch each other, forming eyeballs. Place the eyeball pairs about 1 inch apart. If desired, make some round and some oval. Gently press a black or dark brown candy-coated milk chocolate piece off-center into each mound to make googly eyes. Bake in the preheated oven on two oven racks for 10 minutes. Turn off oven. Let meringues dry in oven with door closed for 40 minutes. Remove from oven; cool completely on cookie sheets. When they're completely cooled, insert the pointed end of a 6- to 8-inch wooden skewer into the bottom center of each meringue. Makes about 48 pairs.

Scaredy-Cat Ice Cream Cake

- 1 15- to 21½-ounce package brownie mix
- ½ gallon chocolate ice cream, softened
- ⅓ cup chocolate cookie crumbs
- 2 blue corn tortilla chips
   Tropical-flavored rolled fruit leather
- 2 large white gum balls
- 1 large orange gum ball
- 3 pieces green apple-flavored licorice twists, halved lengthwise
   Purchased fondant*
   Yellow paste food coloring
   Orange paste food coloring

Line a 13×9×2-inch baking pan with foil, allowing foil to extend over edges of pan; set aside. Prepare brownie mix; bake in the prepared baking pan according to package directions. Cool brownie in pan completely. Use foil to lift brownie from pan onto a cutting board. Remove foil. Using the bottom of a 9-inch springform pan as a guide, cut a circle from brownie. Place the brownie circle in a 9-inch springform pan (eat remaining brownie scraps or save for another use).

Spoon softened ice cream over brownie in pan, spreading evenly. Cover and freeze for 2 hours. Sprinkle cookie crumbs over top of ice cream.

For ears, press in blue tortilla chips. For cat eyes, press a small cutout piece of fruit leather onto each white gum ball; press into cake. Add an orange gum ball for the nose. For whiskers, add green licorice twists, trimming as necessary. For mouth, color about ⅓ cup fondant yellow and another ⅓ cup fondant orange. Alternate 2×½-inch pieces of the colored fondant on a piece of waxed paper, placing the pieces close together. Roll out fondant

Continued on page 138

Spooky Banana-Berry Smoothies

- 2 cups fat-free plain yogurt
- 2 medium ripe bananas, peeled and frozen
- 1 cup sliced fresh strawberries or frozen unsweetened whole strawberries
- 1 cup mixed fresh berries (such as raspberries, blueberries, and/or blackberries) or frozen unsweetened mixed berries
- 1 tablespoon honey (optional)
   Ghostly Meringue Eyes (see recipe, left)

In a blender, combine yogurt, fruit, and, if desired, honey. Cover and blend until smooth. Pour into glasses. Serve immediately with Ghostly Meringue Eyes. Makes 3 or 4 servings.

Witch's Hat Calzones

1 3.5-ounce package sliced pepperoni
½ of an 8-ounce package cream cheese, softened
¼ cup finely shredded or grated Parmesan cheese
2 8-ounce packages (16) refrigerated crescent-roll dough
1 egg, lightly beaten
1 tablespoon water
   Finely shredded or grated Parmesan cheese (optional)
   Dried Italian seasoning (optional)
   Crushed red pepper (optional)
   Pizza sauce, warmed (optional)

Reserve six to eight slices of pepperoni. Chop remaining pepperoni slices. In a small bowl, stir together chopped pepperoni, cream cheese, and the ¼ cup Parmesan cheese until well combined. Set aside.

Preheat oven to 425°F. Lightly grease an extralarge baking sheet; set aside. On a lightly floured surface, unroll each package of crescent-roll dough. Separate dough into individual triangles. Place half the dough triangles on the prepared baking sheet. Place about 1 tablespoon of the pepperoni-cheese mixture in the center of each triangle. In a small bowl, stir together egg and water. Brush triangle edges with some of the egg mixture. Top with remaining triangles. Press triangle edges together to seal. Brush dough with egg mixture. Fold short edges of the dough triangles up, forming a hat brim. Prick the dough a few times with the tines of a fork.

If desired, sprinkle with additional Parmesan cheese, Italian seasoning, and/or crushed red pepper. Cut reserved pieces of pepperoni into small stars, crescent moons, and/or small diamonds. Press onto dough for decoration. Bake in the preheated oven for 8 to 10 minutes or until golden. Serve warm with pizza sauce if desired. Makes 8 calzones.

Continued from page 137

to about ¼-inch thickness. Cut out a "smile" shape; place on cake. Cover and freeze cake until firm, at least 4 hours or up to 24 hours.

To serve, remove sides and bottom of pan and place cake on a platter. Makes 1 cake (12 servings).

*Note: Look for fondant in hobby stores where cake decorating supplies are sold. Or, for a homemade version, prepare Easy Fondant (see recipe under Moody Monsters, opposite).

Scary Skulls

5   medium pears
5   wooden craft sticks
12 ounces white baking chocolate, coarsely chopped
5   3-inch-square plastic-foam blocks or florist's foam
    Assorted small black candies
    Green jelly beans

Wash and dry pears; remove stems. Insert a wooden craft stick into the stem end of each pear.

In a heavy medium saucepan, heat and stir white chocolate over low heat until melted. Hold pears over saucepan using sticks. Spoon melted chocolate evenly over pears, allowing excess chocolate to drip off. Insert the stick of each pear into a foam block.

Let stand about 30 minutes or until chocolate is set.

Decorate pears with candies to resemble skulls, attaching candies with remaining white chocolate (remelting if necessary). Place foam blocks in decorative dishes and top with green jelly beans. Makes 5 skulls.

Tippy Tombstones

1   3-ounce can chow mein noodles (about 1¾ cups)*
1   cup cornflakes
½   cup raisins, snipped dried apricots, dried cherries, and/or dried cranberries
2   cups peanut butter-flavored pieces (12 ounces)
4   ounces white baking chocolate or vanilla-flavored candy coating, chopped
     Red, orange, and/or brown decorating icing

Line an 8×8×2-inch baking pan with foil, allowing foil to extend over edges of pan; set aside. In a large bowl, combine the chow mein noodles, cornflakes, and raisins; set aside.

Put the peanut butter-flavored pieces in a medium microwave-safe bowl.

Microwave, uncovered, on 100% power (high) for 1 minute. Stir until smooth. (If necessary, microwave for 15 to 45 seconds more, stirring after every 15 seconds or until melted. Or place the peanut-butter pieces in a small saucepan; heat and stir over low heat until the pieces are melted.) Pour the melted peanut-butter pieces over the noodle mixture and stir until all of the mixture is coated. Spread mixture into prepared pan, pressing evenly. Cool about 30 minutes or until mixture is set. Use foil to lift mixture from pan onto a cutting board. Remove foil. Use a tombstone-shape cookie cutter to cut shapes, or cut into 3×2-inch rectangles.

Put the white baking chocolate in a small microwave-safe bowl. Microwave, uncovered, on 100% power (high) for 45 seconds. Stir until smooth. (If necessary, microwave for 15 to 45 seconds more,

stirring after every 15 seconds until melted. Or melt white baking chocolate in a saucepan as before.) Lightly spread the fronts, tops, and sides of tombstones with melted white chocolate. Place on waxed paper and let stand about 15 minutes or until set. Decorate with icing. Makes 6 to 8 tombstones.

Note: If desired, use 1¾ cups chow mein noodles from a 5- to 6-ounce can or package for the tombstones and use remaining noodles to make "grass." Place noodles in a large plastic or paper bag; add several drops green food coloring. Close bag and shake to color the noodles. For darker or more even color, add more food coloring and shake again.

★Tip: If tombstones won't stand, prop them up with large gumdrops or other candy.

Moody Monsters

Canned white frosting
Yellow, green, violet, and orange paste food coloring
Purchased miniature banana muffins and/or miniature brownie muffins
Small decorative candies, nonpareils, red fruit leather, jellied orange slices (halved), gumdrops, and/or colored sugars
Purchased fondant or Easy Fondant

Tint frosting with desired color of paste food coloring. Place frosting in small resealable plastic bags; snip off one corner of each bag. Pipe frosting onto muffins as desired for faces and body parts and to attach candies. Press fondant through a garlic press for hair. Form hats by cutting the fruit leather into triangles and then rolling it up, starting from a long end. Or use inverted muffins for hats, securing them with frosting as necessary.

Easy Fondant: Place one 16-ounce can white frosting in a large mixing bowl. Stir in as much powdered sugar as possible and continue adding powdered sugar until you are able to knead mixture into a ball that is not sticky (about 4 cups total). Tint fondant with paste food coloring as desired.

eerie edibles

Imbue your Halloween party food with a playfully spooky attitude. Whether you're going for shivers or laughs, these great-tasting treats will help you scare up a nail-biting, teeth-chattering, giggle-inducing good time.

WRITTEN BY WINI MORANVILLE   PHOTOGRAPHED BY BLAINE MOATS AND MARTY BALDWIN   FOOD STYLED BY DIANNA NOLIN

Boneyard Treats

Your merry band of ghosts and goblins will think you sneaked off to the graveyard to dig up these ghoulish goodies! The trick to these treats is simple—fashion bone-shape graham crackers into peanut-butter sandwich cookies, and then dip them in a vat of candy coating. Looking fresh out of the grave thanks to a little dirtlike dusting of cocoa powder, they'll tickle everyone's funny bone.

Kooky Cauldron Sundae

What's to be found in this troubling bubbling cauldron? Eye of newt and toe of frog? Wool of bat and tongue of dog? Well, more like lime sherbet and gummy worms in a sinfully good chocolate shell. The effect is a little bit batty and all-out yummy. It will make a fantastically freaky finale to your harrowing Halloween gala.

Creepy Crawlers

Watch out—these little cookie critters might just bite back! What doesn't bite, however, is how easy they are to make: Use a can of vanilla frosting with a few stir-ins to decorate purchased cookies, and add edible candies for the "eeeeek!" effect. Even very little hobgoblins can help make these not-so-terrifying treats.

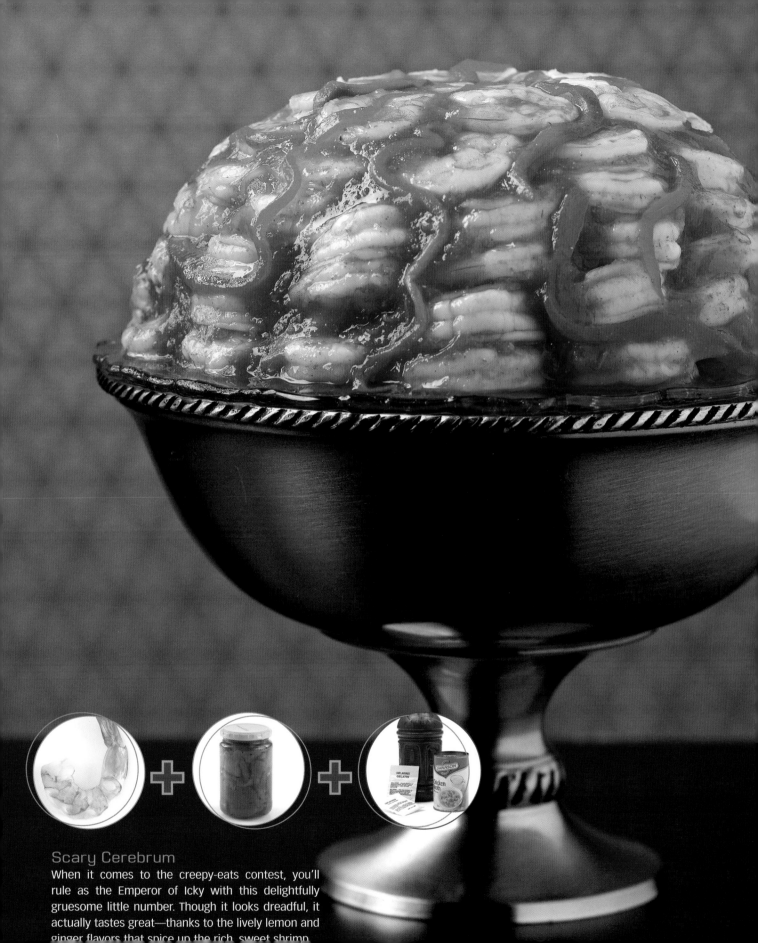

Scary Cerebrum

When it comes to the creepy-eats contest, you'll rule as the Emperor of Icky with this delightfully gruesome little number. Though it looks dreadful, it actually tastes great—thanks to the lively lemon and ginger flavors that spice up the rich, sweet shrimp.

Mad Scientist Wraps

You could concoct a batch of these spooky dudes yourself, but for more fun—and less work—why not let everyone at your party take a turn at playing Dr. Frankenstein? For a creatively creepy time, simply put out the wrap ingredients alongside a few frightening examples, and let guests stuff, jab, and poke their way to their own monstrous models.

Wicked Witch's Hat

Decorate this treat "witch"-ever way you want—to summon up an oddball spirit, go wacky with the crazy hues shown. For something a little more wicked, choose traditional black and orange food coloring pastes. Either way, the popcorn-and-candy snack will hint that a wayward crone has passed by these parts, casting a colorfully crazy spell on your party.

eerie edibles
recipes

Boneyard Treats *page 140*

Peanut butter
Bone-shape graham crackers
Vanilla-flavor candy coating, melted
  according to package directions
Cocoa powder

Spread peanut butter between two graham-cracker bones. Set aside. Dip peanut-butter-filled bones into candy coating. Place on a waxed paper-lined baking sheet; let stand until firm. Lightly dust with cocoa powder if desired.

Mad Scientist Wraps *page 144*

6 7- or 8-inch whole wheat or plain
   flour tortillas
⅓ cup mayonnaise or salad dressing
6 leaves leaf lettuce (optional)
6 slices cooked ham (3 ounces)
6 slices cooked turkey breast
   (3 ounces)
   Assorted decorations such as:
   parsley sprigs, sweet red pepper
   strips, ripe olives, small pimento
   stuffed green olives, small
   pepperoncini peppers, julienned
   carrots, small sweet pickles, and
   shredded lettuce
   Mayonnaise, salad dressing, or
   honey mustard
6 slices American cheese
   Wooden picks

Preheat oven to 350°F. Wrap tortillas in foil and bake for 10 minutes.

Spread each tortilla with 1 tablespoon mayonnaise. Lay a lettuce leaf over mayonnaise, and top with ham and turkey. Roll up and secure with wooden pick. Stuff one end of rolled tortilla with sweet red pepper strips, shredded lettuce, parsley sprigs, and julienned carrots.

Attach olives for eyes and nose and a piece of pepper for the mouth with mayonnaise or honey mustard. Cut an apron shape from the cheese and lay atop tortilla. Add pickles or peppers for shoes; use cheese as a blanket. Makes 6 wraps.

Wicked Witch's Hat *page 145*

20 cups popped popcorn (1 cup unpopped)
1½ cups light-color corn syrup
1½ cups sugar
1   7-ounce jar marshmallow creme
2   tablespoons butter
1   teaspoon vanilla
    Purple and lime-green paste food coloring
    Candy-coated milk chocolate pieces or small hard candies
    Red rolled fruit leather, cut into strips

Line a 12-inch pizza pan with foil. Grease foil and set aside. Remove and throw away all unpopped kernels from the popped popcorn. Grease two 13×9×2-inch or larger baking pans. Divide popcorn evenly between the two pans.

In a large saucepan, combine corn syrup and sugar. Heat over medium-high heat until boiling, stirring constantly. Remove from heat; stir in marshmallow creme, butter, and vanilla. Pour half of this mixture (about 2 cups) into another saucepan. Tint each portion with desired food coloring. Add marshmallow mixture to popcorn (keep colors separate). Stir to coat evenly. Cool until popcorn can be handled easily, about 10 minutes.

With greased hands, press one color of the popcorn mixture into prepared pizza pan. Shape the remaining popcorn mixture into an 8-inch cone about 6 inches in diameter. Top base with cone shape. Decorate with chocolate pieces and fruit leather. Makes one witch's hat.

Make-Ahead Tip: Prepare Wicked Witch's Hat as above. Loosely cover with plastic wrap and store at room temperature for up to 24 hours. If desired, remove "hat" from pizza pan and place on a serving platter.

Scary Cerebrum *page 143*

3   pounds frozen cooked medium
    shrimp (with tails), thawed and
    drained well
¼   cup roasted red sweet peppers,
    cut into ¼-inch thick strips
1   cup chicken broth
1   teaspoon unflavored gelatin
1½ teaspoons finely shredded lemon
    peel
¼   cup lemon juice
3   tablespoons tomato paste
1   tablespoon honey
3   cloves garlic, minced
½   teaspoon salt
½   teaspoon ground ginger
¼   teaspoon cayenne pepper

In a 1½-quart glass bowl (3 inches high, 7½ inches in diameter), begin arranging shrimp, tails toward the center, in a circle to make a flat layer in the bottom of the bowl. (Only the round backs of the shrimp should be visible from the outside of the bowl.) Repeat layers until bowl is full, pressing down every couple layers. As bowl fills up, tuck strips of the roasted red pepper in and around shrimp forming "blood vessels." (It helps to peer through the sides of the glass bowl to adjust as necessary.) When bowl is full, press down firmly with a plate that fits inside the bowl. Set aside.

In a small saucepan, combine chicken broth and unflavored gelatin; let stand 5 minutes. Cook and stir over medium heat until gelatin has dissolved. Whisk in lemon peel, lemon juice, tomato paste, honey, garlic, salt, ginger, and cayenne pepper until combined. Pour mixture over shrimp in bowl. Cover and chill at least 5 hours or overnight.

To unmold, set bowl in a sink filled with warm water for several seconds. Invert a large plate with sides over bowl. Invert plate and bowl together and remove bowl to unmold. Cover and chill until needed (up to 24 hours).

Creepy Crawlers *page 142*

1 16-ounce can vanilla frosting
½ teaspoon orange, cherry, lemon, almond or anise extract (optional)
3 to 3½ cups powdered sugar
Desired color paste food coloring
Small cookies with white filling such as chocolate sandwich cookies, peanut butter sandwich cookies, and/or miniature multicolored vanilla wafers
Black string licorice, jellied orange slices, yellow sprinkles, small decorative candies, and/or multicolored nonpareils

Reserve 3 tablespoons of frosting; cover and set aside. In a medium bowl, combine remaining frosting, desired extract (if using), and 2 cups powdered sugar. Knead in enough of the remaining powdered sugar to make a moderately firm claylike mixture. Divide into portions and knead in desired color food coloring. Keep mixture covered when not using.

Make creative creepy crawlers, using claylike mixture, cookies, and assorted candies. Attach pieces with reserved frosting. Makes 3 to 4 dozen crawlers.

Kooky Cauldron Sundae *page 141*

12 ounces chocolate-flavored candy coating, chopped
6 small balloons
4 ounces vanilla-flavored candy coating, chopped
Green paste food coloring
Lime sherbet
Orange and yellow nonpareils
Orange coarse sugar
Sour gummy worms
Pretzel sticks
Candy pebbles (optional)
Yellow-, orange-, and red-tinted shredded coconut*

Heat chocolate-flavored candy coating according to package directions just until melted, stirring occasionally. Cool candy coating slightly. Meanwhile, inflate balloons to a 4-inch diameter. Carefully dip the balloons into the melted candy coating halfway up the balloon (photo a). (You want chocolate to coat balloon well to form a sturdy cauldron.) If desired, using a thin metal spatula, spread the chocolate coating to evenly coat the balloon. Place balloons on an aluminum-foil–lined cookie sheet. Allow chocolate to run under bottom of balloon for support. Place in the freezer for 20 to 30 minutes or until chocolate coating is very firm. Reserve any remaining chocolate coating to use for patching holes.

Working with one balloon at a time, prick balloon with a straight pin and deflate (photo b). Carefully remove balloon by gently pulling it away from the sides of the chocolate (photo c). Use a small brush to fill in any holes with remaining melted chocolate candy coating. Return to freezer.

Melt 2 ounces of the vanilla-flavored candy coating according to package directions. Cool candy coating. Working with one cauldron at a time, use a small brush to apply the melted candy coating to top edge of the cauldron, making drips down the sides. Chill in freezer to set. Melt the remaining vanilla candy coating. Tint melted candy coating with green food coloring. With a small brush, apply melted candy coating to the top edge of each cauldron, allowing coating to drip down the sides. Place in freezer to set.

Cauldrons can be stored in a covered container in the refrigerator for up to three days or in the freezer for up to one month. To assemble, scoop lime sherbet into the cauldrons. (Put cauldrons in freezer if not serving immediately.) Sprinkle with nonpareils and orange sugar and decorate with gummy worms right before serving.

Arrange pretzels on six serving plates to make campfires. If desired, circle pretzels with candy pebbles. Sprinkle with tinted coconut. Set cauldrons on top of pretzel campfires. Makes 6 servings.

Tinted coconut: Place about ¼ cup shredded coconut in a small resealable plastic bag. Add a few drops of the desired liquid food coloring and shake to mix.

TREATS INCOGNITO

As kids, we were told not to play with our food. Moms will toss those rules out when it comes to this selection of goodies!

DESIGNERS: TAMI LEONARD, DIANNA NOLIN   PHOTOGRAPHER: MARTY BALDWIN

We're fun to make, and we are much sweeter than WE LOOK!

Oh YEAH?

Enjoy EYEBALL PIE, *opposite*, complete with black-lace candy eyelashes and a gooey vanilla pudding base. For a creepy display, put the finished treat on top of a shaggy fabric cutout. ANGRY EYEBROWS, *this page*, make yummy companions. The cookies get their name from shredded coconut that has been tinted black and sprinkled over frosted pretzel sticks.

A cheese-and-cracker snack deserves to be dressed up for Halloween. Clever CANDY CORN CRACKERS are made by mounting corn-shape cheese nibbles on crackers with sour cream dip. Stuffed olives and meat slices finish the silly spoof.

What's not to LOVE about DONUTS and chocolate?

Chocoholic Halloween witches, take note of this dressed-for-success WITCH HAT. Made from an ice cream cone dripping with chocolate coating, the pointed headgear sports a hatband of colorful candy-coated gum squares (miniature candies would work, too). The base of a chocolate doughnut makes a treat yummy enough to really sink your teeth into.

Why cut corners? NIBBLE them off INSTEAD.

A trio of ghoulish TOMBSTONE BROWNIES gets an aged granite appearance from a dusting of powdered sugar. The chocolate tombstones are planted in a brownie graveyard with accents of grass made from coconut shavings tossed with green food coloring.

Instead of screams of fright, little snackers will squeal with delight at this sweet and not at all scary HAUNTED HOUSE. Go architectural with toaster pastries and build a snack that includes fudge-stick cookies, pretzels, frosting accents, and petite icing decorations in bat and ghost shapes.

EYEBALL PIE

Shown on *page 148.*

3½-inch graham cracker tart shell
Cherry pie filling
Vanilla pudding
Sealable plastic bag
Kiwi
Black peel-'n-pull lace candy

Spoon *2 tablespoons* of cherry pie filling into the bottom of a tart shell. Carefully spoon *2 tablespoons* of vanilla pudding over the pie filling, spreading to smooth the surface. Place a small amount of pie filling, without cherries, into a resealable plastic bag. Snip a small hole in one corner of the bag and squeeze filling onto the pudding to create bloodshot eyes, referring to the photo on *page 148.* Peel and slice the kiwi. Put one slice onto the center of the pudding. Center a cherry from the pie filling on the kiwi slice. Cut 1-, 2-, and 3-inch-long eyelashes from the black lace candy. Insert the eyelashes into the pudding.

ANGRY EYEBROWS

Shown on *page 149.*

Canned vanilla and chocolate icing
Green or purple food coloring
2×4-inch unfrosted brownie or
  4-inch-diameter sugar cookie
Two mini vanilla wafers or
  one large marshmallow
Two black jelly beans or red hots
One large gum ball or Jujube candy
Black or red peel-'n-pull lace candy
Candy corn (optional)
Black food coloring paste
Small resealable container
Shredded coconut
Pretzel sticks

Use green or purple food coloring to tint some vanilla icing. Frost the brownie or cookie with the tinted icing. Use mini wafers or cut one large marshmallow in half for eyeballs. Place the eyeballs on the brownie or cookie as shown in the photo on *page 149.* Use icing to attach jelly beans or red hots for the pupils. Use a gum ball or Jujube for the nose. Cut a piece of lace candy for the mouth; press it into a frown and add candy-corn teeth if desired.

To make eyebrows, place some black food coloring paste and a few drops of water into a small resealable container; stir to mix. Add coconut, seal the container, and toss to color the coconut. Completely cover two pretzel sticks with chocolate icing. Immediately roll the pretzels in the tinted coconut. Use icing to attach the eyebrows.

TOMBSTONE BROWNIES

Shown on *page 152.*

Two 15- to 23.5-ounce packages
  of brownie mix
Aluminum foil
Powdered sugar
Unsweetened cocoa powder
Canned vanilla and chocolate icing
Purple, black, and green food coloring paste
Resealable plastic bags
Oreo cookie crumbs
Three 4-inch lengths of wooden skewers
Small resealable container
Shredded coconut

Line an 8×8×2-inch and a 9×13×2-inch pan with foil. Prepare each brownie mix according to package directions and bake one mix in each pan following directions. Cool in pans. Use edges of foil to lift and transfer brownies to a cutting board. Remove foil. From the 9×13-inch brownie, cut 1½×3-inch rectangles for tombstones. Trim the top corners off of some of the rectangles.

Combine powdered sugar and a little cocoa powder and sprinkle mixture over the tombstones. Tint small amounts of vanilla icing with black and purple food coloring paste. Place each tinted icing into a resealable plastic bag. Snip a tiny hole in one corner of each bag and squeeze the icing to decorate the tombstones, referring to the photo on *page 152.* Lightly sprinkle tombstones again with the powdered sugar and cocoa mixture.

Frost the top and sides of the 8×8-inch brownie with chocolate icing and sprinkle top with cookie crumbs. Insert about half of a 4-inch length of wooden skewer into the center bottom of three brownie tombstones. Position the skewered-tombstones on the frosted brownie with opposite ends of the skewers. (Place the other tombstones on a platter for people to eat right away!)

For the grass, place some green food coloring paste and a few drops of water into a small resealable container; stir to mix. Add coconut, seal the container, and toss the mixture to color the coconut. Sprinkle the green coconut around the base of each tombstone on top of the graveyard brownie.

HAUNTED HOUSE
Shown on *page 153*.

  Canned vanilla icing
  Cocoa powder
  Yellow food coloring
  Two toaster pastries (we used Frosted Brown
    Sugar Cinnamon Pop-Tarts)
  Honey graham cracker
  Mini pretzel sticks
  One chocolate snack stick (we used Double
    Chocolate Pop-Tart Snak-Stix)
  Candy pumpkin
  Two fudge stick cookies
  Black decorating gel
  Mini or petite bats and ghost icing decorations

Use cocoa powder to tint some icing brown and yellow food coloring to tint some icing yellow. Use a sharp knife to diagonally cut one toaster pastry in half and secure one half to the second toaster pastry with brown icing for the roof.

From the graham cracker, break off one rectangle for the door and cut two 1-inch squares for the windows. Frost the windows with yellow icing. Attach the windows and the door with brown icing. Attach 1-inch lengths of pretzel sticks along the vertical edges of the windows for the shutters. Attach a snack stick and a candy pumpkin on the door. Use brown icing to secure a fudge stick cookie at the bottom of the house for the step and at the top of the roof for the chimney. Use black gel to pipe the windowpanes and to add squiggle lines over the house. Use icing to attach bat and ghost decorations.

CANDY CORN CRACKERS
Shown on *page 150*.

  Block of cheddar cheese
  Block of Colby-Jack cheese
  Block of provolone or mozzarella cheese
  Triangle-shape crackers, such as
    Triscuit Thin Crisps
  Purchased dairy sour cream dip

Cut blocks of cheeses into $1/4$-inch-thick slices. Cut the slices into triangles the size of the crackers. Cut each triangle of cheese into thirds. Spread dip on the tops of the crackers. Arrange the cut cheese pieces on the crackers to resemble candy corn.

WITCH HAT
Shown on *page 151*.

  2 ounces semisweet chocolate
  Chocolate-rolled sugar ice cream cone
  Candy pumpkins
  Waxed paper
  Purchased unfrosted plain or chocolate
    cake doughnut
  Canned chocolate icing
  Nonpareils or sprinkles
  Orange, yellow, and green Starburst candy or
    candy-coated gum (we used mini Chiclets)

Melt semisweet chocolate according to the package instructions. Holding the open end of the cone, dip the bottom half at an angle into the melted chocolate. Immediately press candy pumpkins into the chocolate. Place the cone on waxed paper and let sit until the chocolate sets.

Frost the top and side surfaces of a doughnut with icing. Sprinkle icing with nonpareils or sprinkles. Center the open end of the cone on the frosted doughnut. Use a sharp knife to cut candies or gum pieces into quarters and adhere them around the bottom of the hat with icing.

EYEBALL PIE

what's
BREWING?

Halloween partygoers will happily slurp these festive—and delicious—drinks. Concoct nonalcoholic beverages, perfect for costumed guests of any age, or adults-only drinks with added spirits.

FOOD STYLIST: DIANNA NOLIN
PHOTOGRAPHER: MARTY BALDWIN

Silly but not so scary touches on chilled drinks stir up extra fun at any Halloween get-together. From left to right: DRACULA'S SODA, GHOUL-ADE, WHITE GHOST, and LAYERED OOZE.

DRACULA'S SODA

Garnish the ice cream sodas with gummy teeth and cherry "eyeballs" on straws. Shown on *page 156*.

- 2 to 3 scoops vanilla ice cream
  Carbonated water, chilled
- 3 tablespoons fruit punch concentrate, thawed

Place ice cream in two tall 10-ounce soda glasses. Fill glasses with ½ to ¾ cup carbonated water. Drizzle thawed fruit punch concentrate over ice cream. Serve immediately. Makes 2 servings.

GHOUL-ADE

This ghoulishly smooth drink tastes like cream soda. Shown on *page 156*.

- 1 8-ounce carton vanilla yogurt
- ½ teaspoon unsweetened lemon-lime- or orange-flavored powdered soft drink mix
- 2 tablespoons honey
- 1 cup carbonated water, chilled

In a medium bowl, mix yogurt with lemon-lime- or orange-flavored soft drink mix and honey.

Cover and chill for 2 hours or overnight. Just before serving, gently stir in carbonated water for fizz. Ladle into glasses. Makes 2 (8-ounce) servings.

WHITE GHOST

Use blueberries to create a haunting face in this rich and frothy drink. Shown on *page 157* and at *right*.

- 1 6-ounce can unsweetened pineapple juice, chilled
- ¼ cup cream of coconut
- 1 cup lemon-lime carbonated beverage, chilled
- ¼ cup half-and-half or milk
- 1½ cups crushed ice
  Blueberries (optional)

In a blender container, combine pineapple juice, cream of coconut, lemon-lime beverage, half-and-half, and crushed ice; cover and blend until smooth.

Pour into three glasses. If desired, garnish with blueberries to form a ghostly face through the glass. Serve immediately. Makes 3 (8-ounce) servings.

LAYERED OOZE

Pretty to look at and just as refreshing to sip, this citrus medley will become a favorite party drink for all age groups. Freezing the juice mixtures keeps the slushy layers separated. Shown on *page 157* and *below*.

- 3 tablespoons frozen grape juice concentrate
- 1½ cups water
- 3 tablespoons frozen orange juice concentrate, partially thawed
- 3 tablespoons frozen limeade concentrate, partially thawed
- 1 drop green food coloring
- 2 cups lemon-lime carbonated beverage or carbonated water, chilled

In a small mixing bowl, combine the grape juice concentrate and ½ *cup* of the water. Pour mixture into a 1½-quart glass baking dish.

In another small bowl, combine the orange juice concentrate and ½ cup water. Pour mixture into another 1½-quart glass baking dish.

In a third small mixing bowl, combine the limeade concentrate, the remaining ½ cup water, and 1 drop green food coloring. Pour mixture into a third 1½-quart glass baking dish. Cover and freeze the mixtures for 4 to 24 hours or until firm.

WHIITE GHOST AND LAYERED OOZE

To form slush mixtures, remove each dish from the freezer. Break up each frozen mixture with a wooden spoon. Scoop *one-fourth* of the grape juice mixture into each of four chilled 10-ounce glasses. Scoop *one-fourth* of the limeade mixture over the grape mixture in each glass. Spoon *one-fourth* of the orange juice mixture over the limeade mixture in each glass.

Slowly pour $\frac{1}{2}$ *cup* of the lemon-lime carbonated beverage down the sides of each glass. If desired, stir gently to mix. Makes 4 servings.

BLOODY SCARY HARRY

For the additional ice cubes, freeze part of an ice cube tray with some extra vegetable juice to keep from diluting your drink. Shown at *right*.

  ¾ cup hot-style vegetable juice, chilled
  2 tablespoons vodka
  2 teaspoons lime juice
     Dash celery salt
  ½ cup ice cubes
     Ice cubes (optional)
     Bottled hot pepper sauce (optional)
     Small carrot with top (optional)
     Star anise (optional)
     Long shreds of beet (optional)

In a blender, combine vegetable juice, vodka, lime juice, and celery salt; add $\frac{1}{2}$ cup ice cubes. Cover and blend until smooth. If desired, fill a glass with additional ice cubes. Pour drink into glass. Season to taste with hot pepper sauce.

If desired, garnish with a small carrot with green top. For a scary face, press a small piece of star anise into the carrot. For hair, drape long shreds of beet over carrot top. Makes 1 (8-ounce) serving.

SHRUNKEN-HEAD MARTINI

This basil-laced martini will have you smiling along with the shrunken head sitting on the edge of the glass. Shown at *right*.

     Ice cubes
  3 ounces vodka
     Dash vermouth
     Basil leaves
     Shrunken-Head Skewer

Fill a cocktail shaker with ice; add vodka, vermouth, and two basil leaves. Shake vigorously; strain and pour mixture into martini glass. Add additional basil leaves. Garnish with Shrunken-Head Skewer. Makes 1 serving.

Shrunken-Head Skewer: Cook a boiling onion in boiling water, covered, for 3 minutes; drain and cool. Remove outside skin from onion. Press whole cloves into onion to form a face. Thread onion onto a 6-inch skewer with almond-stuffed green olives to form the shrunken head with arms.

Create the smiling shrunken head for SHRUNKEN-HEAD MARTINI, *below left,* from a small onion, whole cloves, and stuffed green olives. Tangles of shredded basil complete the drink, adding whimsy and flavor. Our dramatic BLOODY SCARY HARRY, *below right,* displays a ghoulish star-anise face and long locks made from beet shreds.

SHRUNKEN-HEAD MARTINI
AND BLOODY SCARY HARRY

outdoor decor

Whether you prefer to be the scariest house on the block or a kid-friendly stop along the trick-or-treating route, you'll find the perfect Halloween scheme among this collection of outdoor decorating ideas.

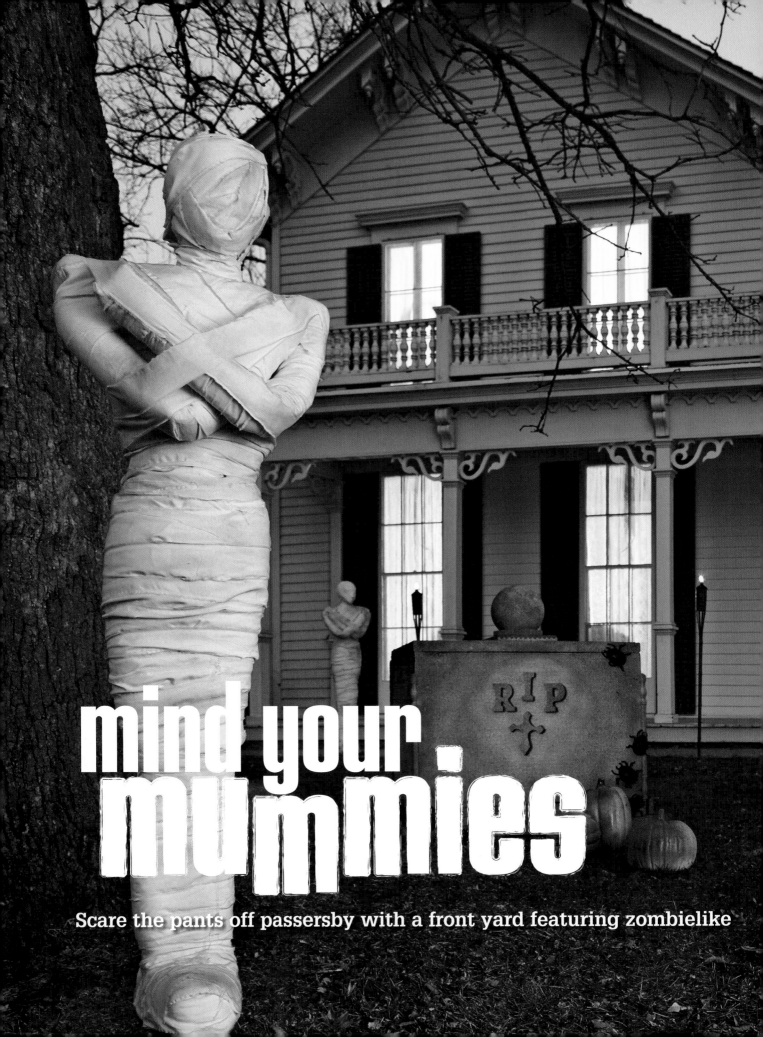

mind your mummies

Scare the pants off passersby with a front yard featuring zombielike

Set the stage for terror

by arranging simple-to-swaddle sculptures amid time-battered-looking headstones and crypts. Having sloughed off their mortal casings, dirt-stained mummies escape their vaults to haunt this spine-chilling tableau. These mummies may seem menacing, but there's nothing intimidating about their construction. T-shaped plywood frameworks form skeletons for muslin-covered batting and wig-head skulls.

Pay tongue-in-cheek tribute to those who have gone before with tombstones cut from plastic-foam planks. Finish the markers with specialty stone paints, and add humorous epitaphs to curb the fear factor. Fashion a not-so-final resting place by constructing a statuesque crypt from a cardboard carton, plastic-foam planks, and wooden and foam embellishments.

Every high-quality Halloween display requires a few creepy crawlies. Marshal a parade of scarab beetles—Egyptian symbols of immortality—across the crypt. Sculpt these scavengers from plastic-foam eggs enhanced with dimensional paint, chenille-stem legs, and antennae bent to simulate motion.

Promote an air of decay by scattering plastic-foam tomb remnants, tipped-over urns, and gray-painted pumpkins about the scene. Toss dirt on the mummies' shoulders for a recently exhumed effect. Light the torches, set the ghostly exhibit aglow, and watch the goose bumps rise!

mummies that eerily rise to haunt the twilight-lit landscape.

PRODUCED BY PATRICIA GARRINGTON AND HOLLY RAIBIKIS   WRITTEN BY ANN WILSON   PHOTOGRAPHED BY GREG SCHEIDEMANN

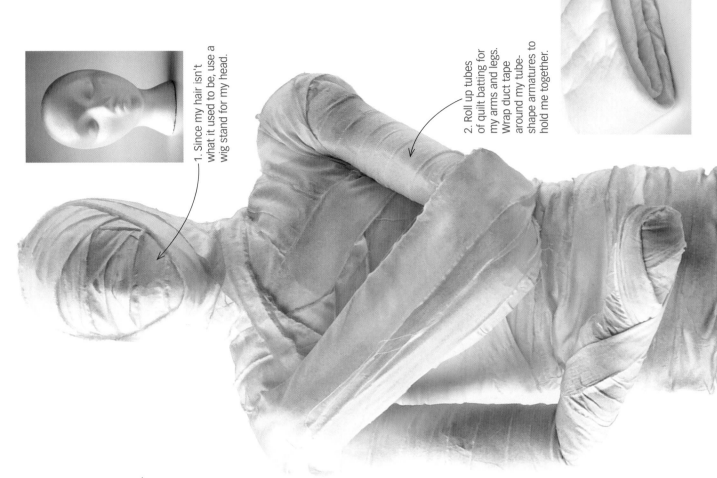

1. Since my hair isn't what it used to be, use a wig stand for my head.

2. Roll up tubes of quilt batting for my arms and legs. Wrap duct tape around my tube-shape armatures to hold me together.

The Anatomy of a Mummy

MATERIALS

For 1 full-figure mummy:

12×14-inch piece of ½-inch-thick plywood for base

4 angle braces

40-inch length of 2×2-inch lumber for body brace

(**Note:** For the half-figure mummy, sharpen one end of this length into a point.)

12-inch length of 2×2-inch lumber for shoulders brace

2 strap braces

Drill

10-inch length of ½-inch-diameter dowel

Wig form

Glue gun and hotmelt adhesive

King-size quilt batting

2½ yards of 40-inch-wide muslin

Duct tape

Two 22-inch lengths of heavy wire

Polyester fiberfill (*optional*)

Khaki spray paint

Floral spray paint (We used Design Master Glossy Woodtone.)

For 1 half-figure mummy:

You'll need all of the materials listed above for the full-figure mummy, but omit the plywood base, and angle braces.

INSTRUCTIONS

Referring to the diagram, *below*, fasten one end of the 40-inch length of lumber to the plywood base using angle braces on all four sides.

Referring to the diagrams, center the 12-inch length of lumber (the shoulder brace) on top of the body brace, forming a T-shape; fasten with strap braces on the front and back.

Drill a ¼-inch hole in each end of the shoulder brace. Drill a ½-inch hole in the center top of the shoulder brace. Push one end of the wooden dowel into the wig-form neck opening and secure with glue.

For the legs, cut two 27×36-inch pieces of quilt batting and two matching

3. Then wrap pieces of muslin fabric around my body.

4. Tear lots of muslin strips. From top to bottom, hot-glue the strips all over me.

5. Spray a century or two of age on me by randomly spraying my body with translucent paints.

pieces of muslin. Lay one piece of batting on a flat surface and roll it into a 27-inch-long tube. Lay the tube on one piece of muslin and roll it to cover the batting. Secure the muslin with glue. Repeat for the other leg.

For the arms, cut two 22×36-inch pieces of quilt batting and two matching pieces of muslin. Roll into tubes and cover with muslin as instructed for the full-figure mummy legs. Push one piece of wire through the center of each arm tube, allowing the wire to extend beyond one end.

Using scrap quilt batting and muslin, make two 5-inch-long foot tubes.

Stand the leg tubes side by side on the plywood base with the body brace between them. Secure with duct tape at the hips, knees, and ankles. Wire the arms to the shoulder brace.

For the body, measure and cut two or three pieces of quilt batting and one piece of muslin that are shoulder-width and long enough to extend from the tops of the legs in front, up over the shoulders, and down to the tops of the legs in the back. Lay the body pieces over the shoulders and secure with duct tape at the waist. Stuff the body area with scraps of batting or fiberfill to achieve the desired look. Use scissors to clip a hole in the batting and muslin at the center top of the shoulder brace. Push the end of the wooden head dowel into the center hole in the shoulder brace and glue in place.

Cut the remaining muslin fabric into 2-inch-wide strips and wrap the mummy as desired, securing the strips with glue.

Spray the mummy with khaki and wood-tone paints to distress as desired.

For one-half mummy: Assemble as directed for the full-figure mummy, omitting the base, legs, and feet.

Body cover

Wig head
Dowel
Arm tube
Wire
Arm tube
Leg tube
Leg tube
Foot tubes

Hole
Strap brace
Angle braces

Crypt

MATERIALS

Large cardboard carton (Ours measured 22×36×27 inches.)
Serrated knife
1½-inch-thick and/or 2-inch-thick plastic-foam planks
Bamboo skewers
Gray latex paint and paint roller
10-inch-diameter plastic-foam ball
12-inch-diameter plastic-foam ring
5-inch-tall wooden letters
8-inch-tall wooden cross
Zigzag-edge wooden trim
2 wooden corner guards, cut in half
Glue for plastic foam (We used Styroglue.)
Faux-stone spray paint (We used Krylon Make It Stone!
    18202 Charcoal Sand and 18201 Black Granite.)
Floral spray paint (We used Design Master Glossy Wood Tone.)

INSTRUCTIONS

Using a serrated knife, cut rectangles from the foam planks as follows: two side rectangles to fit the sides of the cardboard box; a front and a back that measure the box height by the box length plus the thickness of the foam sides.

Measure the top of the box and cut the crypt top from a plastic-foam plank. For the base, cut two plastic-foam pieces larger than the crypt top and in graduating sizes. *Note:* We cut the base pieces from different plank thicknesses. Also, cut a 15×15-inch plastic-foam square for the decorative top assembly.

Use gray latex paint and a roller to base-coat the crypt pieces. Assemble the crypt around the box, using skewers to hold the pieces together. Again using skewers, attach the plastic-foam top and the plastic-foam base pieces to the box.

Cut the wooden trim to fit around the 15×15-inch square, and glue the pieces in place. Assemble the decorative top, gluing the ring to the center of the square and attaching the ball to the center of the ring using skewers. Attach the decoration to the top of the crypt with skewers and glue. Glue the letters, cross, and corner guards in place. Apply faux-stone spray paints to the crypt; let dry completely. Spray the wood-tone paint on the edges to age the crypt.

See Scarab Beetles instructions, *opposite.* Glue the beetles to the crypt.

Tombstones

MATERIALS

Serrated knife

1½-inch-thick plastic-foam planks

Gray spray paint

Black acrylic paint

Paintbrush

11-inch tall wooden cross

Faux-stone spray paint (We used Krylon Make It Stone! 18202 Charcoal Sand and 18201 Black Granite.)

Glue for plastic foam (We used Styroglue.)

Floral spray paint (We used Design Master Glossy Wood Tone.)

INSTRUCTIONS

Using a serrated knife, cut tombstones from the plastic-foam planks, referring to the photos, *page 163* and *below,* for design inspiration. (Ours measure about 18×30 inches.)

For the "Help Me!" tombstone: Spray-paint the tombstone gray, leaving some of the white foam unpainted to further distress the piece.

Lightly spray the tombstone, using both colors of granite spray paint.

Add the words with a paintbrush and black paint.

Finish the tombstone with wood-tone paint, randomly spraying it over the piece.

For the tombstone with the cross: Glue the wooden cross to the front of the foam shape. Paint the tombstone as directed above, spraying more granite paint on the cross for design emphasis.

Scarab Beetles

MATERIALS

For 2 beetles:

Plastic-foam egg in the desired size

Serrated knife

Crafts knife

Black acrylic crafts paint

Paintbrush

Glossy decoupage medium

Brown dimensional slick paint

Black chenille stems

Scissors

Glue gun and hotmelt adhesive

INSTRUCTIONS

Cut the plastic-foam egg in half lengthwise with a serrated knife. Using a crafts knife, cut a V-shape wedge out of each side near the small end of each egg half, forming the beetles' necks.

Paint the beetles with black acrylic paint; let dry. Then paint the beetles with two or three coats of gloss decoupage medium, allowing it to dry between coats. Squeeze thin lines of brown slick paint to distinguish the head from the body and the wings.

For legs, cut six pieces of chenille stem for each beetle. Cut two short chenille-stem lengths for antennae. Push one end of each leg into the underside of each beetle's body and bend outward. Drop a bit of glue on each leg where it joins the body. After the glue has dried, bend the legs, referring to the photos, *above.* Insert antennae into the front of each head and bend as desired.

WITCH IS IN!

Boo-ti-ful
Yards

Why limit your holiday decor to carved pumpkins? Arm yourself with clever turns of phrase, a few supplies, and your trusty glue gun to turn the great outdoors into a Halloween masterpiece.

PHOTOGRAPHER: MARTY BALDWIN   DESIGNER: LORI HELLANDER

The Witch Is In

No self-respecting witch goes anywhere without her broom. Let trick-or-treaters know she's home with a sign, *opposite,* made from a precut wood plaque and a gold glitter paint pen, proclaiming her availability for casting spells or stirring up brews. (If you don't trust your lettering skills, use the instructions for the stair risers, *page 174,* and attach computer-created words to the plaque.) Create a ghoulish broom by adding green raffia or dried grasses to one end of a weathered stick. Cinch an old leather belt around the end and this witch's broom is ready to take flight.

As Bats fly 'round the Moon,

GO a-Haunting,

Halloween is Soon!

Halloween Is Soon

A natural twig wreath and a gazing ball transform an ordinary birdbath into a crystal ball on a stand. But to get a glimpse into the future, guests first have to look past simple construction-paper bats perched on twisted strands of black and orange chenille stems.

THERE?

GOES

WHOOOOOO

Who Goes There?

Whether perched on a porch or parked on the steps, this wise trio of birds stands guard against the season's ghouls and goblins. Gleaming crescent moons add sparkle; for a spookier atmosphere, paint the moons and owls in glow-in-the-dark paint or sprinkle the figures in opalescent glitter.

Change the MESSAGE on the STAIR risers to tie in with your HALLOWEEN party theme.

Come in

& Sit

A Spell

Come In and Sit a Spell
Guests will feel right at home with this friendly invitation—until they realize they've been bewitched! Use a spooky Halloween font like Chiller or Jokerman to create the words on wood-pattern paper. For stability, paste the printed paper onto balsa and tack the pieces to the wooden steps. To decorate concrete steps, affix the phrase with double-stick removable poster tape.

Enter if You Dare
This witch's hat, crafted in black with accents of bright orange and purple, is a jaunty holiday signal to passersby. Use ribbons to tie it to your front gate or to hang it from your door. The directions provide a guideline for the words, but don't be afraid to use your imagination to match the hat to your own bewitching welcome.

The Witch Is In!
shown on *page 168*

MATERIALS
5-foot length of 6-inch-diameter tree branch

2- to 3-feet-tall and 10-inch-diameter bunch of purchased dried grass

Glue gun and hotmelt adhesive

Rubber bands (optional)

Packaging tape

2-inch-wide strip of black leather or an old leather belt

Two 30-inch-long leather shoelaces

5×16-inch wooden plaque with hanger

Gold glitter paint pen

INSTRUCTIONS
Remove most of the smaller branches from the large tree branch, leaving a few at the top. Shorten the remaining branches; one shortened branch will serve as a hook for the plaque.

Hot-glue dried grass several inches from the bottom end of the branch. Secure the grass with rubber bands or packaging tape 2–3 inches below the top edge of the grass. Wrap the leather strip or belt around the broom to cover the rubber bands or tape; cut the leather so the ends overlap by 1–2 inches, and tape. Wrap leather shoelaces around the leather strip to crisscross on the front side; tack in place on the back with hot glue. Hot-glue the overlapped area together to fit snugly on the broom.

Referring to the photograph, *page 168*, use the gold glitter paint pen to write the message on the wood plaque; let the paint dry. To hang the plaque, loop the plaque's hanger over one of the shortened branches.

Halloween Is Soon
shown on *page 169*

MATERIALS
Computer and printer

Three 8½×11-inch sheets of orange paper

Double-stick tape

10-inch-diameter white gazing ball

5 sheets of clear laminating paper

Pinking shears

Tracing paper

Black construction paper

Chenille stems: 2 each of black and orange

Glue gun and hotmelt adhesive

Natural wreath sized to fit the birdbath and gazing ball

Spray adhesive

White glitter

Birdbath

INSTRUCTIONS
Type a poem or phrase of your choice in a font of your choice on a computer, adjusting the font size so the words are about 1 inch tall. Format the text so each line of the poem or phrase is centered on a page; adjust the print orientation to landscape. Print each line onto a sheet of orange paper.

From the printed sheets, cut three 1¾×11-inch strips with a line of the poem or phrase centered on each strip. From the scraps, cut 8 additional 1¾×11-inch blank orange strips. Make one long strip with the blank strips, using double-stick tape to slightly overlap the short ends. Wrap the long strip three times around the gazing ball, referring to the photograph, *page 169*. Plan the positions of the poem or phrase lines and mark the locations on the wrapped strip. Remove the strip from the gazing ball and secure the lines to the long strip with double-stick tape. Laminate the entire strip, following the manufacturer's instructions. Trim the long edges with a pinking shears. Reposition the laminated strip on the gazing ball and secure with double-stick tape.

Trace the bat pattern, *page 177,* onto tracing paper;

Cut out the pattern. Draw around the pattern three times on black construction paper; cut out. Laminate the bats and cut out the laminated shapes. Twist together the orange and black chenille stems in pairs. Hot-glue one end of a twisted chenille stem pair to the center back of each bat, allowing most of the stem to extend below the bat.

Spray the top side of the wreath with adhesive. Immediately sprinkle glitter over the adhesive; let dry. Place the wreath in the birdbath, top side up, and center the gazing ball on the wreath. Stick the chenille stems with attached bats into the wreath. Tape a third bat to the top of the ball.

Who Goes There?

shown on *page 170*

MATERIALS

Graph paper (optional)
Three 12×18-inch sheets of stiff black felt
12×18-inch sheet of white crafts foam
8½×11-inch sheet of white felt
Spray adhesive
White glitter
Glue gun and hotmelt adhesive
Three 18-inch lengths of ¾-inch diameter
  wooden dowel
Black acrylic paint
Paintbrush
Computer and printer
8½×11-inch sheets of white
  computer paper
8½×11-inch sheets of lime-
  green card stock

INSTRUCTIONS

Enlarge the owl/moon pattern on *page 176* using graph paper or a photocopier; cut out the pattern. Use the pattern to cut three owls/moons from stiff black felt. Cut along the edges of the owl pattern to make separate patterns for the two moon sections; also cut out the two eye patterns. Cut three of each moon section from white crafts foam and cut three pairs of eyes from white felt. Spray one side of each white-foam moon section with adhesive, reversing the side of one set so it

is in the opposite direction, as shown in the photo on *page 170*. Immediately sprinkle white glitter onto the adhesive; let dry.

Hot-glue the glittered moon sections onto the corresponding sections of the black felt owl. Hot-glue the eyes on the owl faces. Paint the dowels black; let dry. Hot-glue the top 6 inches of a dowel to the back side of each owl so about 12 inches extend below the figure.

Use a computer to make the three wording tags. Print a test sample on white typing paper. When satisfied, print the tags on lime-green card stock. Cut out the tags and hot-glue one to each owl. Insert the bottom end of the dowels into the ground.

(If wet weather is a concern, laminate the paper and felt before assembling the project.)

Come In and Sit a Spell

shown on *page 171*

MATERIALS

Computer and printer
8½×11-inch sheets of wood-pattern
  scrapbook paper
Three 4×36-inch pieces of balsa wood
Spray adhesive
12 decorative tacks

INSTRUCTIONS

Type the message in the font of your choice on a computer, adjusting the font size so the words are no more than 3½ inches tall. Format the text so each individual word will be centered on a page. If necessary, adjust the print orientation to landscape so the text runs in the same direction as the wood grain on the paper. Print each word onto a sheet of wood-pattern paper.

Cut the printed sheets into 4×11-inch strips, centering each word on a strip. Position the words on the balsa pieces, referring to the photograph on *page 171*. Cut additional 4-inch-wide strips of wood-pattern paper with the grain running the length of the strips to completely cover the balsa. Spray adhesive onto the back of the strips and smooth into place on the balsa.

Use decorative tacks to mount the signs on the stair risers.

(If wet weather is a concern, laminate the paper before assembling the project.)

Enter if You Dare

shown on *page 172*

MATERIALS

Graph paper (optional)

20×30-inch piece of black foam-core board

12×12-inch sheets of card stock: 2 orange and 1 black

Crafts knife

Sandpaper block

Permanent black marker

Spray adhesive

12×12-inch sheets of scrapbook paper: 2 each of stripes and dots

Ribbon: 1/3 yard of 3/4-inch-wide orange and 2 yards each of 1-inch-wide black grosgrain, 1-inch-wide black picot-edge, and 1-inch-wide orange satin

Glue gun and hotmelt adhesive

1/4-inch hole punch

Pop dots

INSTRUCTIONS

Enlarge the hat pattern on *page 177* onto graph paper or use a photocopier; cut out the pattern. Draw around the hat pattern on foam-core board and cut out with a crafts knife. Type the words "Enter If You Dare" in the font of your choice on a computer, adjusting the font size so the words are no more than 3½ inches tall. Print out the letters on orange card stock; cut out.

Sand the cut edges of the foam-core hat smooth with the sandpaper block. Color the cut edges with the permanent black marker. Spray the front side of the hat with adhesive. Smooth sheets of dotted paper onto the brim and striped paper onto the upper hat. Turn the hat over and trim away the paper along the edges of the hat. Center the 3/4-inch-wide orange ribbon over the line where the striped and dotted papers meet; hot-glue in place, securing the ends on the back of the hat.

Spray the back of the letters for the word "Enter" with adhesive and mount onto the sheet of black card stock, leaving about ½ inch between each of the letters as you adhere the orange letters to the black card stock. Create a shadow behind these letters, cutting the black card stock even with the edges of the orange letters in some areas and varying the width of the shadow from 1/16 inch to 1/4 inch in other areas. Referring to the photograph *below* for placement, arrange the letters for "Enter" on the top portion of the hat as shown.

Use striped paper scraps to decorate the remaining letters for the words "If You Dare," cutting stripes for the letters of "You Dare" and using the hole punch to make dots for the letters of "If." Mount the stripes and dots on the letters with spray adhesive. Referring to the photograph *below* for placement, arrange the letters on the front of the sign and adhere them with pop dots.

Cut the remaining ribbons into 1-yard lengths. You will have six lengths of ribbon (two each of orange, black picot-edge, and black grosgrain). Hot-glue one of each ribbon to the back side of the hat, in line with the top edge of the brim. Tie a knot 2½ to 3½ inches from the opposite end of each ribbon length. Use the ribbons to tie the sign in place.

(If wet weather is a concern, laminate the paper and foam core before assembling the project.)

WHO GOES THERE? OWL/MOON PATTERN

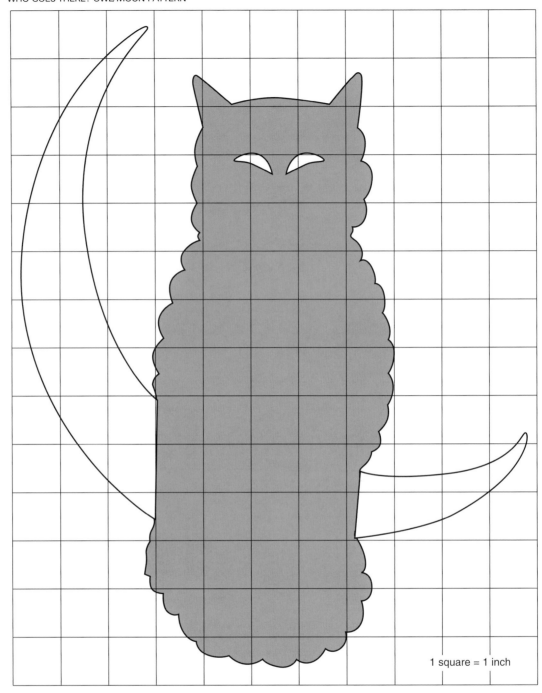

1 square = 1 inch

ENTER IF YOU DARE WITCH HAT PATTERN

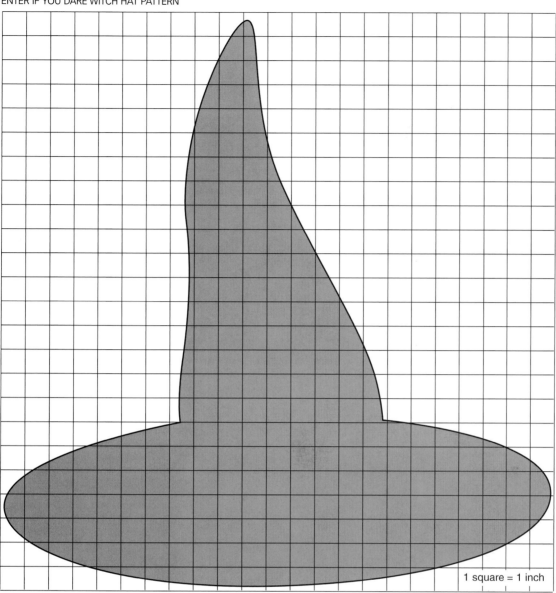

1 square = 1 inch

HALLOWEEN IS SOON BAT PATTERN

It's time for the bewitching belles of Halloween to party! With a little "witchcraft" you can dress your own house for a GHOULISH GALA.

Welcome to the
WITCHES'
DEN

DESIGNED BY PATRICIA GARRINGTON
WRITTEN BY AMY LEIBROCK
PHOTOGRAPHED BY CAMERON SADEGHPOUR

The Witching Hour
Set the stage for a spooky soirée with warm, glowing light. Candles line the path; a lighted grapevine garland frames the porch; and dark witch, ghost, and bat silhouettes, cut from black paper, are illuminated from inside the house.

Spooky
Specials

Spells..............5 bat wings

Potions.........3 dragon teeth

Incantations........4 frog legs

Prices good through October 31.

Spellbinding Soup

It takes very little toil and trouble to make this cauldron bubble. This witch's brew starts with spray-foam insulation that's left to dry and then painted green. Kids will have fun embellishing it with rubber toads, lizards, and other critters.

Lots of Shadows

Shadowy silhouettes of bats and witches having a cackling good time will cast an aura of black magic on the festivities. Use our patterns, or draw your own using a white pencil on heavy black paper.

Spooky Shimmer

Light the way with a path of flickering luminaries, *top left*, dressed for the occasion with stars punched out of black paper with a crafts punch.

Bewitching Bats

Every witch needs a sidekick. Some prefer cats and others like bats, as long as they're dark and scary. Round out your guest list with furry bats and spiders, *top right* and *above right*, made by covering foam eggs and balls with simple crafts supplies.

Eerie Address

You can't expect witches to feel at home on Songbird Street or Butterfly Avenue. Mark the party with a spookier address, *above right,* using a wooden house-number sign, paint, and rubber stamps.

Creepy-Crawly Displays

Gather all the ingredients—eyeballs, newts, worms, and other creepy crawlies—needed to concoct a potent witch's brew. They'll look perfectly icky displayed in glass apothecary jars, *above left*.

Playful Parking

When you're hosting a gaggle of witches, they'll need a place to park their brooms, *right*. Whip up your own brooms by wrapping twigs and grass around wooden dowels. Mark the "parking lot" with a sign made by printing on iron-on transfer paper and ironing it onto a painted stretched artist's canvas.

Silhouettes

MATERIALS

Heavy, rolled black crafts paper
Scissors
White pencil
Double-stick adhesive tape

INSTRUCTIONS

Copy and enlarge the patterns to the desired size. Cut out the patterns and trace them onto black paper using a white pencil. Cut out silhouettes. Attach the silhouettes with tape.

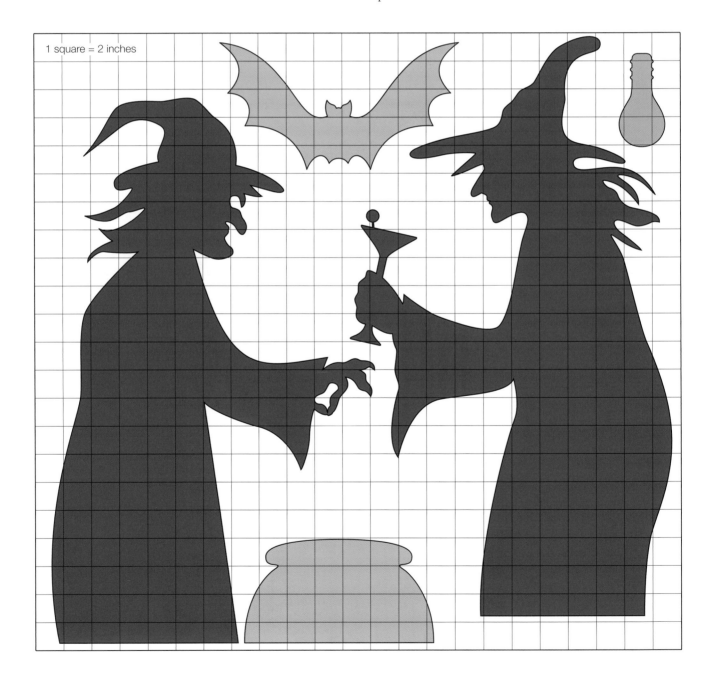

1 square = 2 inches

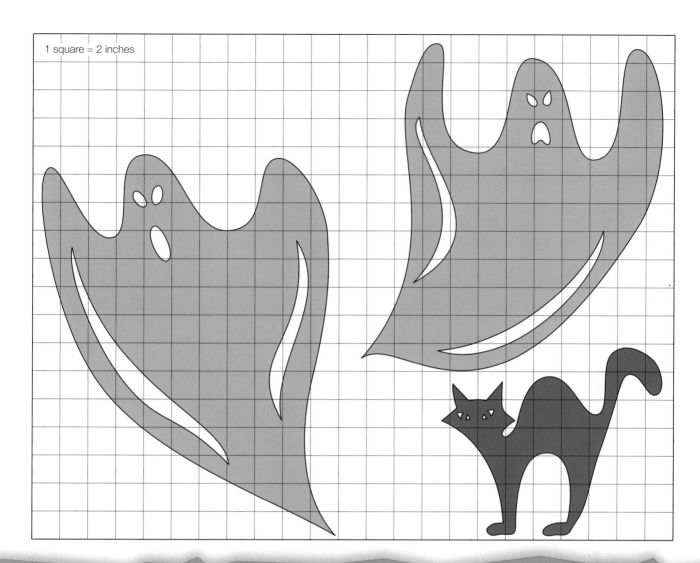

1 square = 2 inches

Bubbling Cauldrons

MATERIALS

Plastic cauldrons: one large and one medium
Flowerpot saucer the same diameter as the large
   cauldron opening
Aluminum foil
2 cans of spray-foam insulation for large cracks (We used
   Great Stuff.)
Assorted rubber critters such as toads, lizards, rats, and bats
Plastic eyeballs
Crafts knife
Lime-green acrylic crafts paint and paintbrush

INSTRUCTIONS

For the large cauldron, line the saucer with aluminum foil. Spray foam insulation into the tray until it's just a little more than full. Let the wet foam set up for about 10 minutes to form the "bubbling brew," and then insert rubber critters and plastic eyes as desired.

On a separate sheet of aluminum foil, spray small blobs of the foam insulation. Use these blobs as decorative "drips" to glue on around the edge of the large cauldron.

For the medium cauldron, cut a hole large enough for the cauldron to lie flat on its side. Protect a flat working surface with aluminum foil and lay the cauldron on its side. Spray foam insulation into the container, letting the foam extend beyond the opening to create a "spill."

Let all foam insulation dry for 36 hours to cure.

After the foam in the saucer has completely set, remove the foam from the saucer and peel off the foil. Set the "bubbling brew" into the opening of the large cauldron. Trim to fit using a crafts knife. Peel the foil from the underside of the medium cauldron's "spill."

Paint all areas of the "bubbling brew" with a wash of lime-green paint and water. Avoid painting the critters. Add more critters on the surface of the brew if desired.

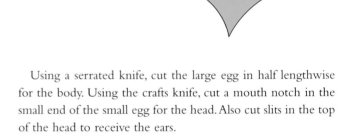

Bat Ear

Bat Wing

Furry Bats

MATERIALS

For 1 bat:

Tracing paper
Pencil
Scissors
Black crafts foam for ears: 2×3-inch rectangle
Black interfacing: 12×12-inch square
4 black chenille stems
Glue gun and hotmelt adhesive
Serrated knife
Large foam egg for the body: 6-inch-diameter
Small foam egg for the head: 3-inch-diameter
Crafts knife
Black acrylic crafts paint and paintbrush
12×12-inch square of loopy chenille fabric or fantasy fur
Round wooden toothpick
2 red quilter's ball-head pins

INSTRUCTIONS

Trace the patterns, *above right,* onto tracing paper and cut out. Cut the ears from black crafts foam and the wings from interfacing.

Using the wing pattern as a guide, form and cut lengths of chenille stem to outline the wings and make ribs. Glue in place and let dry. Set the ears and wings aside.

Using a serrated knife, cut the large egg in half lengthwise for the body. Using the crafts knife, cut a mouth notch in the small end of the small egg for the head. Also cut slits in the top of the head to receive the ears.

Paint all surfaces of the head and body halves black. Let the paint dry thoroughly.

Sandwich the wings between the body halves, and glue in place. Let dry. Cover the body with chenille fabric, and glue in place.

Glue the head to the body, using a toothpick to help position and hold the head in place. Glue the ears into the head slits. Insert the pins for eyes.

1313 Witch Lane Sign

MATERIALS

Wooden house-number sign
Acrylic crafts paints: orange, purple, and black
Paintbrushes
Rubber-stamp set (We used The Paper Studio by Stampabilities, 62 pc. Chisel #J-04-95171.)
Fine-grit sandpaper
Acrylic spray sealer

INSTRUCTIONS

Base-coat the entire sign with orange. Let dry. Paint the outside frame with purple; let dry.

Stamp the letters and numbers with black. Let dry. Using a fine paintbrush, add a thin black outline about ⅜ inch from the inner edge of the frame.

Sand the edges of the frame with fine-grit sandpaper for an aged look. Seal the sign with acrylic spray sealer; let dry.

Witches' Brooms

MATERIALS

- Wooden dowel (1-inch-diameter, 36-inch-long), tree branch, and bamboo branch (each about 36 inches long) for broom handles
- Lavender acrylic crafts paint
- Paintbrush
- Fine-grit sandpaper
- Willow twigs, bamboo, and decorative grass for broom brushes
- 3 pieces of black interfacing fabric: 2×10-inch strips
- Raffia and twine
- Scissors
- Glue gun and hotmelt adhesive

INSTRUCTIONS

Paint the wooden dowel with lavender acrylic paint. Let dry. Sand with fine-grit sandpaper for a worn look.

For each broom, choose the brush material you want. Lay the material across one length of interfacing fabric so that about the top 2 inches of brush material extend beyond the fabric; glue in place. Let dry. Wrap one end of the gathered brush material around one end of the broom handle, gluing it in place. Let dry.

Referring to the photo, *page 181,* wrap raffia or twine several times around the top of each broom brush, and glue in place.

Spooky Specials and Witch Parking Only Signs

MATERIALS

- Stretched artist's canvases: 14×18×1½ inches and 9×12×3 inches
- Acrylic crafts paints: beige and dark brown
- Paintbrush
- Acrylic glaze medium
- Plastic wrap
- Acrylic spray sealer
- Iron-on transfer paper for computer

INSTRUCTIONS

Base-coat the fronts and sides of the stretched canvases with beige. Let dry.

Mix a glaze using glaze medium and dark brown acrylic paint. Brush the glaze over the canvas. While it's still wet, dab the canvas with a crumpled piece of plastic wrap to create the effect of crinkled parchment. Leave the corners and edges darker than the center. Let dry. Spray with sealer.

Use a computer and word-processing software to set up and print the lettering onto computer iron-on transfer paper.

Iron the lettering transfer onto the signs following the manufacturer's instructions.

Furry Spiders

MATERIALS

For 2 spiders:

- Plastic-foam ball for heads: 1½-inch-diameter
- Plastic-foam ball for bodies: 3-inch-diameter
- Serrated knife
- Crafts knife
- 2 toothpicks
- Black acrylic crafts paint
- Paintbrush
- 4 green quilter's ball-head pins
- 8 black jumbo chenille stems
- Glue gun and hotmelt adhesive
- Black feather boa: 36-inch

INSTRUCTIONS

Cut the 1½-inch plastic-foam balls in half using a serrated knife. Lay the flat edges of the heads on a cutting surface. Using a crafts knife, cut out a curved section from each head so the head curve smoothly fits the body curve.

Insert a toothpick halfway into each head and centered in the neck curve. Push the rest of the toothpick into a body, aligning the flat sides. Add glue to secure the heads to the bodies; let dry. Paint the spiders with black acrylic paint; let dry.

For eyes, push the ball-head pins into the heads at the fronts.

Cut the chenille stems in half. Push one end of each leg into the underside edge of each spider body and bend outward. Drop a bit of glue on each leg where it joins the body. After the glue has dried, bend each leg at the knee and foot.

Cut two 9-inch lengths from the black feather boa for each spider. Glue one length in a spiral on the back of each spider and the other length on the tummy of each.

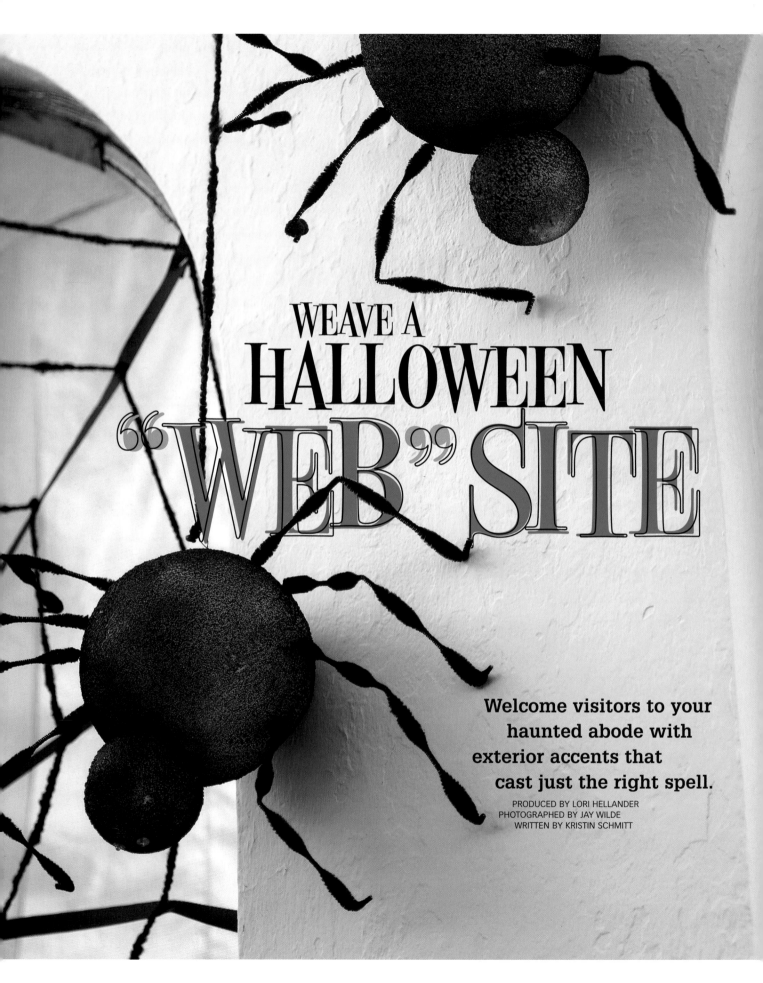

WEAVE A HALLOWEEN "WEB" SITE

Welcome visitors to your haunted abode with exterior accents that cast just the right spell.

PRODUCED BY LORI HELLANDER
PHOTOGRAPHED BY JAY WILDE
WRITTEN BY KRISTIN SCHMITT

Simple Spiders
Some of the easiest crafting projects are the most effective. These magnificently monstrous spiders, *opposite,* are easily crafted from foam balls, black spray paint, and chenille stems.

Window Webs
Lengths of black ribbon and yarn and a little strategic weaving (if a spider can do it, surely you can, too!) are all it takes to add shadowy webs to your front windows. Dangle a couple crawling critters from the roofline to complete the creepy picture.

WHILE DRY LEAVES CRUNCH UNDER FOOT AND A BRISK BREEZE

hints of Old Man Winter's calling, we observe October 31 with a final encounter in the outdoors. Trick-or-treaters embark on a tour of the neighborhood in search of treats dispensed at the nudge of a doorbell. Old movies frighten us with haunting images of dark and gloomy house fronts. Play into the spirit of the season by dressing up your own home's exterior with a few black and orange decorations and some of the holiday's favorite icons.

Everyone loves to hate the creepy sensation of creatures crawling about. And nothing says excitingly eerie like a house overrun with murky cobwebs. So play up the part of the neglected mansion with oversize spiderwebs and a couple plump inhabitants fixed in your front windows. Scraggly, leafless artificial trees perched in the yard accentuate the deserted ambience, while strings of orange lights wrapping the skeletal branches add a gruesome glow.

After adorning the facade with hints of haunted inhabitation, you can summon partygoers and trick-or-treaters up the front walk with a few friendlier accents. Break with tradition by opting out of carved pumpkin faces this year. Instead, outline your walk with towering pumpkin topiaries that are fun to paint and stack. Finish by outlining the walkway with lengths of plastic garden fencing.

For our easy instructions on how to make these wicked-fun spiders, webs, and topiaries, turn to page 190.

Potted Pumpkins
Summer blooms may have faded, but don't winterize the decorative planters yet. Urns and planters make a perfect base for pumpkin topiaries; embellish the towers with bits of garden moss tucked around the pumpkins.

Happily Haunting Entry

The walk to the front door takes on a pumpkin-patch look when pumpkins are stacked and displayed in towering arrangements lining the walkway.

Sensational Stacks

Use wooden dowels—in Halloween colors, of course—to securely stack pumpkins into formation. Opt for artificial pumpkins if you plan to reuse your towering masterpieces next year.

AN EERIE-SISTIBLE ENTRANCE ENTICES TRICK-OR-TREATERS AND OTHER GUESTS IN A MERRY-NOT SCARY-WAY.

Simple Spiders

MATERIALS

For each spider:

Crafts-foam balls: one 6-inch-diameter and one 3-inch-diameter
1 bamboo skewer
Black matte-finish spray paint
2 corsage pins with red heads
8 black bump chenille stems
Heavy gauge florist's wire
Hanging cord

INSTRUCTIONS

To assemble each spider, insert a skewer through a large crafts-foam ball and then into a small crafts-foam ball. Cover your work surface and thoroughly spray the assembled spider with paint. Let dry and spray again if needed. Insert corsage pins into the small ball for the eyeballs. For the legs, insert 4 chenille stems into each side of the spider body. Bend each leg at a 90-degree angle approximately halfway down the length of the chenille stem. Bend the tip of each chenille stem to create the feet.

Cut an 8-inch length of wire for each spider and bend the wire in half; twist the wire several times to form a loop. Insert the ends of the wire into the top of the spider's body. Thread a hanging cord through the loop.

Potted Pumpkins

MATERIALS

For one topiary:

Fresh pumpkins or artificial carvable pumpkins: 1 each in small, medium, and large
Black acrylic crafts paint
Assorted artist's paintbrushes
Matte-finish acrylic spray varnish
Apple corer
36-inch length of 1-inch-diameter wooden dowel
Large garden urn filled with potting soil
Florist's moss

INSTRUCTIONS

Use a pencil to sketch four vertical rows of diamond shapes onto the medium-size pumpkin, using the photograph, *page 188*, as a guide. Using an appropriate-size brush, fill in the diamond shapes with black acrylic paint; let dry. Apply a second coat if necessary. Let dry. Spray the acrylic varnish on all pumpkins and let dry.

Use the apple corer to make holes in the tops and bottoms of the large- and medium-size pumpkins. Make a hole in the bottom of the small pumpkin. Insert the dowel completely through the large pumpkin, then completely through the medium pumpkin, finally placing the small pumpkin on top. Set the pumpkin assembly in the urn, pressing the dowel into your potting soil. Stuff florist's moss atop and below the pumpkins.

Sensational Stacks

MATERIALS

For one topiary:

Fresh pumpkins or artificial carvable pumpkins: 1 small and 1 medium
Acrylic crafts paint: black and orange
Assorted artist's paintbrushes
24-inch length of 1-inch-diameter wooden dowel
Matte-finish acrylic spray varnish
Apple corer
Small urn filled with potting soil
Black electrical tape
Paper fringe: orange and black
Purchased spider

INSTRUCTIONS

Use a pencil to sketch diamond shapes onto the small pumpkin, using the photograph, *page 189*, as a guide. Using an appropriate-size paintbrush, fill in the diamond shapes with black acrylic paint; let dry. Paint the wooden dowel orange and let dry. Apply a second coat if necessary. Let dry. Spray acrylic varnish on both pumpkins and the dowel. Let dry.

Use the apple corer to make holes in the top and bottom of the medium-size pumpkin. Make a hole in the bottom of the small pumpkin. Insert the painted dowel completely through the medium pumpkin, and

then push the small pumpkin onto the top of the wooden dowel. Place the assembly into the urn.

Cut pieces of electrical tape and wrap it around the dowel to create stripes. Decorate with paper fringe and set the purchased spider on top of the bottom pumpkin.

Window Webs

MATERIALS

For a 54×60-inch window:

Tape measure
Cardboard large enough to fit dimensions of web
Black blanket binding (2 packages)
Straight pins
Crafts glue
5 yards of 1-inch-wide satin ribbon
Nubby black yarn
Small tacks or nails

INSTRUCTIONS

For a rigid surface to lay out the web, cut out a rectangle of cardboard 4 inches larger all around than the window measurement. Cut a piece of blanket binding for each side of the window. Arrange the blanket binding pieces on the cardboard, using straight pins to hold the binding in place on the cardboard frame. Glue the binding edges together at the corners. For the spokes of the web, cut lengths of ribbon to crisscross across the frame. Insert ribbon ends into the binding openings, apply glue, and pin in place until dry.

To create the web design, weave yarn between the ribbon spokes, gluing and pinning it to the ribbons at intersections. Let dry. Tack into place around the window.

Wood pieces—Lara's Crafts, www.larascrafts.com to find a retailer.
CUPCAKES
Silicone baking cups, jack-o'-lantern lollipop mold #2113-1704—Wilton Industries, www.wilton.com.

ULTIMATE PARTY GUIDE
pages 80–105
Pattern papers—Rumble Tumble from One Heart…One Mind, www.oneheart-onemind.com.
Modeling clay—Sculpey, www.sculpey.com for a retailer.
Adhesive—Perfect Glue, www.perfectglue.com (available at crafts, fabrics, and hardware stores).
Chalk ink—Colorbox (available at crafts and scrapbooking stores).
Basket die-cut—AccuCut (available at crafts and scrapbooking stores).

TREATS INCOGNITO
pages 148–155
Wilton Industries (tube decorator icings, black), www.wilton.com.

WHAT'S BREWING
pages 156–159
Monster Lounge highball glass (sold individually or in an assorted set of 4)—Seasons of Cannon Falls, 800/377-3335.

MIND YOUR MUMMIES
pages 162–167
Transparent wood-stain floral spray paint—Design Master Glossy Wood Tone, www.dmcolor.com (available at crafts stores).
Make it Stone! Textured spray paint—Krylon, www.krylon.com for a retailer.
Styrofoam wig head—www.costumeuniverse.com.
Plastic foam sheets—provided by FloraCraft (available at crafts stores).

WELCOME TO THE WITCHES' DEN
pages 178–185
BUBBLING CAULDRONS
Spray-foam insultation—Great Stuff, www.greatstuff.dow.com (available at hardware and home improvement stores).
1313 WITCH LANE SIGN
The Paper Studio 62-pc. Chisel #J-04-95171 rubber-stamp set—Stampabilities, www.stampabilities.com.
Iron-on transfers for ink-jet printers—June Tailor Print 'n Press, www.junetailor.com. Stretched canvas (available at crafts stores).

WEAVE A HALLOWEEN "WEB" SITE
pages 186–190
Chenille bump yarn—available at crafts stores.

Note: All products were available at time of publication.

For general information about our other products and services, please contact our Customer Care Department within the United States at (800) 762-2974, outside the United States at (317) 572-3993 or fax (317) 572-4002.

Wiley also publishes its books in a variety of electronic formats. Some content that appears in print may not be available in electronic books. For more information about Wiley products, visit our web site at www.wiley.com.

ISBN 978-0-470-50396-6

Printed in the United States of America

10 9 8 7 6 5 4 3 2

sources

Many of the materials and items used in the projects of this book are available at fabrics, crafts, and department stores. For more information about the products or to find a retailer near you, contact the manufacturers listed below.

PUMPKIN GALLERY
pages 20–31
ARTIFICIAL CARVABLE PUMPKINS AND CARVING SETS—MacJac Enterprises, www.funkins.com.

OUT OF YOUR GOURD
pages 32–41
PUMPKIN MASTERS CARVING SETS—Pumpkin Masters, www.pumpkinmasters.com.
X-ACTO KNIFE AND CARVING SETS—Hunt Corp., 800/879-4868; www.hunt-corp.com.
RUSTED-IRON JACK-O'-LANTERN STAND—Nancy's Metal Art; www.nancysmetalart.com.
ARTIFICIAL CARVABLE PUMPKINS—MacJac Enterprises, www.funkins.com.

GRINNING GOURDS
pages 42–47
STEVE STEININGER—The Potters Ltd., P.O. Box 575, Altoona, IA 50009-0575, 515/967-5226; e-mail: sydmax@att.net; www.thepottersltd.com.

HALLO-WEDDING
pages 50–61
BLEEDING CANDLES—Spirit Halloween, www.spirithalloween.com.
Cake pillars—Wilton, www.wilton.com.
Plastic skeletons—Petite Pete Skeleton, www.scienceartandmore.com.
XOXO ribbon—Adornit, 435/563-1100.
NUT CUPS
Hand silk-screened rub-ons alphabet—Hambly Screen Prints, www.hamblyscreenprints.com.
NAIL-IN-THE-COFFIN PARTY FAVOR
Coffin die cut—AccuCut Box #18 (available at crafts and scrapbooking stores).
Press-on letters—Reminisce Font Buffet (Chicken King), www.designsbyreminisce.com.
Candy mold—two-mold skeleton set, www.candyplus.net.
Spiderweb Lampshade
Lamp—Seasons of Cannon Falls, www.seasonsofcannonfalls.com for a retailer.
Giant spiderweb hand silk-screened acetate—Hambly Screen Prints, www.hamblyscreenprints.com.
Invitation, guest book, pen holder, and groom's corsage Patterned papers, bits-n-pieces sheet, card stock, and rub-ons—One Heart...One Mind, 913/681-6745; www.oneheart-onemind.com.
TABLETOP CHANDELIER
FloraCraft Styro Wonder Cutter Plus, plastic foam—provided by FloraCraft (available at crafts stores).

SPRAY PAINT—Krylon, www.krylon.com for retailers.
PEN HOLDER
Chalk ink—Colorbox (available at crafts and scrapbooking stores).

FAMILY-STYLE FRIGHT NIGHT
pages 62–69
Table runner, pitcher, black-and-white and orange-pattern plates—Target, www.target.com.
CAKE STANDS AND CROWS—Seasons of Cannon Falls, 800/377-3335; www.seasonsofcannonfalls.com for your nearest retailer.
BIRDHOUSES—Hobby Lobby, www.hobbylobby.com for your nearest retailer.
SIGN PAPERS
Shadow-Box scrapbook paper—Michaels, www.michaels.com for your nearest retailer.
White pumpkins—The Salem Collection, 800/289-5006.
Paper bags, sparkly black fun foam, sparkly felt, twigs (we painted black), precut door fun foam shapes (for invitation)—Michael's, www.michaels.com for your nearest retailer.

PUMPKIN PATCH PARTY
pages 70–79
PUMPKIN LUNCH BOX
Circle tin totes #20-7012—Provo Craft, www.provocraft.com for a retailer.